Logic

The methods of logic are essential to an understanding of philosophy and are crucial in the study of mathematics, computing and linguistics. Greg Restall's *Logic* is a comprehensive introduction to the major concepts and techniques involved in the study of logic, including propositions and arguments, truth tables, tree methods, conditionality and natural deduction. Restall explores both formal and philosophical logic and examines the ways in which we can achieve good reasoning.

'The text is wonderfully clear. I recommend it enthusiastically.' Michael Hallett, *Department of Philosophy, McGill University*.

Greg Restall is Associate Professor in Philosophy, Melbourne University, Australia.

Fundamentals of Philosophy
Series editor: John Shand

This series presents an up-to-date set of engrossing, accurate and lively introductions to all the core areas of philosophy. Each volume is written by an enthusiastic and knowledgeable teacher of the area in question. Care has been taken to produce works that while even-handed are not mere bland expositions, and as such are original pieces of philosophy in their own right. The reader should not only be well informed by the series, but also experience the intellectual excitement of being engaged in philosophical debate itself. The volumes serve as an essential basis for the undergraduate courses to which they relate, as well as being accessible and absorbing for the general reader. Together they comprise an indispensable library of living philosophy.

Published:
Greg Restall
Logic

Richard Francks
Modern Philosophy

Dudley Knowles
Political Philosophy

Piers Benn
Ethics

Alexander Bird
Philosophy of Science

Stephen Burwood, Paul Gilbert and Kathleen Lennon
Philosophy of Mind

Colin Lyas
Aesthetics

Alexander Miller
Philosophy of Language

Forthcoming:
Suzanne Stern-Gillet
Ancient Philosophy

Logic
An introduction

Greg Restall

McGill-Queen's University Press
Montreal & Kingston • Ithaca

ISBN 978-0-7735-2422-4 (bound)
ISBN 978-0-7735-2423-1 (pbk)

Legal deposit fourth quarter 2005
Bibliothèque nationale du Québec

Published simultaneously in the European Union
by Routledge, an imprint of the Taylor & Francis Group.

Library and Archives Canada Cataloguing in Publication

Restall, Greg, 1969–
      Logic : an introduction / Greg Restall.

(Fundamentals of philosophy)
Includes bibliographical references and index.
ISBN 978-0-7735-2422-4 (bound)
ISBN 978-0-7735-2423-1 (pbk)

      1. Logic–Textbooks. I. Title. II. Series.

BC108.R47 2005a   160   C2005-904309-1

Typeset in Century Schoolbook and Futura by
RefineCatch Limited, Bungay, Suffolk, England
Printed and bound in Great Britain by
TJ International Ltd, Padstow, Cornwall

To my teachers,
and to my students.

Contents

Acknowledgements

Many people have contributed to this book. I thank my students, who never fail to come up with new insights each time I teach this material. Two students from my 1998 class, Alicia Moss and David Wilson, went above and beyond the call of duty in collating embarrassingly long lists of errors in the early drafts of this manuscript. I owe special thanks to James Chase, who used a draft of this text in an introductory logic course and who provided many of the exercises and examples. My research assistant Robert Anderson helped find some errors and infelicities of expression in the final draft.

I thank my own teachers, especially Rod Girle, Graham Priest and John Slaney. They will each find some of their ideas and attitudes reflected in this text. I will be pleased if I am as able to inspire and enthuse others as my teachers have been able to inspire and enthuse me. Finally, thanks to my family: First, to Christine Parker, whose love and companionship has taught me more than I can express in words. Second, to Zachary Luke Parker Restall, who has been learning to reason just as I have been finishing writing this book.

Greg Restall
The University of Melbourne
greg@consequently.org
March 2003

Introduction

For the student

There are many different reasons to study logic. Logic is the theory of *good reasoning*. Studying logic not only helps you to reason well, but it also helps you *understand* how reasoning works.

Logic can be done in two ways – it can be *formal* and it can be *philosophical*. This book concentrates on *both* aspects of logic. So, we'll be examining the techniques that logicians use in *modelling* good reasoning. This 'modelling' is formal and technical, just like the formal modelling you see in other disciplines, such as the physical and social sciences and economics.

The philosophical aspects of logic are also important, because we try not only to model good reasoning, but also to understand *why* things work the way they do – or to understand why things *don't* work. So, we will not only learn formal techniques, we will also *analyse* and *interpret* those techniques.

So, the techniques of logic are *abstract* and *rigorous*. They're abstract, since we concentrate on particular properties of

1

reasoning that are relevant to our goals. They're rigorous, since we try to define all of the terms we use, and we take our definitions seriously. The goal is for us to *understand* what we are doing as much as possible.

The techniques of formal logic can be used in many different ways. The things we learn can be applied in philosophy, mathematics, computing, linguistics, and many other domains. Logic is important for *philosophy* as reasoning and argumentation form a core part of philosophy. Logic is important in *mathematics* because the formalisation of logic is important when it comes to the study of mathematical theories and mathematical structures: in fact, many of the techniques we will be looking at arose in the study of mathematics. Logic is important in *computing* because the process of describing a problem or process to be implemented in a computer is a problem of formalisation. Furthermore, the kinds of algorithms or recipes we use in solving problems in logic are useful in problems that can be found in computing. Logic is important in *linguistics* because the formal languages used in the study of logic provide helpful models for linguistic theories.

So, logic has its place in many different disciplines. More generally even than that, learning logic helps you to learn how to be precise and rigorous in any area of study.

This book is a self-contained introduction to logic. You should not *have* to read anything else in order to get a well-rounded introduction to logic. However, other books will complement the introduction you will find here. Here are some useful books that complement the approach to logic I have taken. (Numbers in square brackets are references to entries in the bibliography.)

- *Logic with Trees*, by Colin Howson [12] is an introductory text that also uses trees as its fundamental tool in introducing logical consequence. It complements this text nicely: use Howson's book for different explanations of trees and how they work.
- *Beginning Logic* by E. J. Lemmon [15]. This is an excellent introductory text. It is probably the best introduction to truth tables and natural deduction in print (despite being over 30 years old). Lemmon's approach concentrates on natural

deduction (introduced in our Chapter 7) instead of truth tables and trees, which we use here.

- *First-Order Logic* by Raymond Smullyan [29] is a more technical book than this one. If you are interested in seeing more of what can be done with trees, this is the book to use.
- *Thinking About Logic* by Stephen Read [21] is a helpful approach to the philosophical issues discussed in this course, and many more besides.
- *Modern Logic* by Graeme Forbes [6] is a longer book than this. It is also an introduction to logic that incorporates formal and philosophical issues. I recommend it to students who want to explore issues further.
- *Intermediate Logic* by David Bostock [2] covers similar ground to this book, but in more depth. If you wish to explore the issues here further, Bostock's book is a good guide, once you are familiar with the basic concepts of this text. (Unlike Forbes, Bostock presumes you have a basic grasp of formal logic.)
- *Computability and Logic* by George Boolos and Richard Jeffrey [1] is an advanced text that covers material on computability, the fundamental theorems of first-order (predicate) logic (such as Gödel's incompleteness theorems, compactness and the Löwenheim–Skolem theorems), second-order logic and the logic of provability.
- *A New Introduction to Modal Logic* by George Hughes and Max Cresswell [13] is an introduction to modal logic, the logic of necessity and possibility, discussed in Chapter 6.
- My book *An Introduction to Substructural Logics* [22] gives an introduction to relevant logics (and logics like them) that are mentioned in Chapters 6 and 7. It is a great deal more technical than this book.

I hope you find this text a useful introduction to logic!

For the instructor

There are *many* books on logic. The distinctive aspect of this book is its integrated nature as both formal and philosophical. It

3

introduces students to the flavour of current work in logic in the early twenty-first century. This text is flexible; it can be used in many ways. Here are just a few of the ways the text can be used in teaching an introductory logic unit.

- *A term of 8–10 weeks*: Use Chapters 1–4 to introduce propositional logic and Chapters 8–10 for an introduction to predicate logic. These chapters constitute the formal core of the book. Alternatively, if you want to give the students an introduction to the formal and philosophical study of logic, you could use Chapters 1–7.
- *A semester of 12 or 13 weeks*: Use Chapters 1–4 and 8–10 as the formal skeleton of the course, and use as many of the other chapters as you desire to fill in the philosophical implications. I have found (teaching this material both at Macquarie University and at the University of Melbourne) that adding Chapter 5 *Vagueness and Bivalence*, Chapter 6 *Conditionals*, Chapter 11 *Identity and Functions* and Chapter 13 *Free Logic* makes a good single-semester course. Other chapters can be added instead to suit local conditions.
- *A full year*: Use the whole book. This can be done flexibly, with the formal core and some extra chapters used as the main curriculum, with other chapters used as the basis for optional extra assignment work. Each of the 'optional' chapters comes with a number of references that can be used for extra reading.

I am convinced that logic is best studied by keeping the formal and philosophical aspects together. Logic is not a completed science, and teaching it as if it is one gives students the mistaken impression that all of the important issues have been decided and all of the important questions have been given definitive answers. This is a misrepresentation of the state of the art. Interesting issues arise not just at the far-reaching abstractions of advanced mathematical logic, but also at the fundamental issues covered in an introductory course. It is good to bring these issues out in the open, not only so that students get a truer picture of the state of the discipline, but also so that they might be attracted to study the area further!

This book has many influences. My approach to the formal

account of propositional and predicate logic stands in the heritage of Raymond Smullyan [29]. The technique of trees (or tableaux) for predicate logic is suited to an introductory text for a number of reasons.

- Unlike most other proof systems, trees are mechanical. Natural deduction systems and their relatives usually require you to have a 'bright idea' to complete a proof. With trees, bright ideas undoubtedly help, but they are not necessary. Grinding through the rules will invariably yield a result if one is there to be had.
- Trees give you simple soundness and completeness proofs. The Lindenbaum Lemma is not required to provide a complete and consistent set of sentences, with witnesses for quantifiers; out of which you make an interpretation. The set of sentences and the witnesses for the quantifiers are given by the tree method itself. This means that an introductory text can state and prove soundness and completeness results in a manner intelligible to the introductory student. This is important, as soundness and completeness arguments are at the heart of logic as it is actually studied.
- Trees, contrary to much popular opinion, do formalise a nat- ural way of reasoning. Traditional 'axiom and rule' systems formalise the demonstration of validity by taking various assumptions as given, and providing rules to get new truths from old. The argument is valid if the conclusion can be derived from the premises and the axioms, by way of the rules. This is an important style of reasoning, but it is not the only one. Trees formalise another style, which could be called the explication of possibilities. To test to see if an argument is valid, you assume that the premises are true and that the con- clusion is not true, and you explore how this might be. If there is no way for this to happen, the argument is valid. If there is some possibility, the argument is not. This is just as much a style of reasoning as by 'axioms and rules'.

The approach to trees used here is also used in Bostock's *Inter- mediate Logic* [2] and Howson's *Logic with Trees* [12], so students can refer to these books for more examples.

Solutions to the exercises in this text are not printed in the book, but are available on the World Wide Web at the following address:

http://consequently.org/logic/

This means that students can look up solutions for themselves, so it would be unwise to set these exercises for assessment. If you would like help in writing other questions for assessment in a unit based on this text, contact me at greg@consequently.org. Of course, I also welcome any comments or suggestions to help improve the content of this book.

I hope you find this text a useful introduction to logic!

Logic is many things:
a science, an art,
a toy, a joy,
and sometimes a tool.
– Dorothy Grover and Nuel Belnap

PART 1
Propositional logic

Chapter 1
Propositions and arguments

Logic is all about *reasons*. Every day we consider possibilities, we think about what follows from different assumptions, what would be the case in different alternatives, and we weigh up competing positions or options. In all of this, we *reason*. Logic is the study of good reasoning, and in particular, what makes good reasoning *good*.

To understand good reasoning, we must have an idea of the kinds of things we reason about. What are the things we give reasons for? We can give reasons for doing something rather than something else (these are reasons for *actions*) or for liking some things above other things (these are reasons for *preferences*). In the study of logic, we do not so much look at these kinds of reasoning: instead, logic concerns itself with reasons for *believing* something instead of something else. For beliefs are special. They function not only as the *outcome* of reasoning, but also as the *premises* in our reasoning. So, we start with the following question: What are the sorts of things we believe? What are the things we reason with?

Propositions

We will call the things we believe (or disbelieve) *propositions*. The particular name is not important here, but the distinction between propositions and other sorts of things is important. We *express* propositions by using sentences. If I ask you what I believe about something, you will most likely respond by using some sentence or other. Of course expressing propositions is but one of the things we do with sentences. We do lots of other things with sentences too – we ask questions, we express feelings, desires and wishes, we command and request. In the midst of this diversity, the acts of stating and believing are central to the practice of reasoning, so propositions are at the heart of reasoning and logic. We are interested in claims about the way things are, and reasons for them, so propositions, which express how we take things to be, or how we take things not to be (or which express matters upon which we are undecided), are the focus of logic.

We will illustrate the difference between sentences that express propositions and those that do not by exhibiting the contrast. Here are some examples of sentences expressing propositions:

> I am studying logic.   If you like, I will cook dinner tonight.
> Queensland has won the Sheffield Shield.
> The moon is made of green cheese.   Most wars are horrible.
> $2 + 7 = 9$.   The mind is not the brain.
> Euthanasia is justifiable in some circumstances.
> There's no business like show business.   That hurts!

Each sentence in this list is the kind of thing to which we might assent or dissent. We may agree or disagree, believe or disbelieve, or simply be undecided, about each of these claims.

The following sentences, on the other hand, do not express propositions:

> Go away! Please pass the salt.   Hello.
> What is the capital of Tanzania?   Ouch!

These sentences do not express propositions – they are not *declarative*, as they are not the sort of thing that we can believe or disbelieve, or reason with. These parts of speech perform other functions, such as expressing emotions, greeting, asking questions or making requests.

We express propositions to describe the way things are (or, at least, to describe how things seem to us). Propositions are the sorts of things that can be true or false. Our descriptions are successful, or they are not. In the study of logic, we are interested in relationships between propositions, and the way in which some propositions can act as reasons for other propositions. These reasons are what we call arguments.

Arguments

In everyday situations, arguments are dialogues between people. In logic, we do not study all of the features of these dialogues. We concentrate on the propositions people express when they give reasons for things. For us, an argument is a list of propositions, called the *premises*, followed by a word such as 'therefore', or 'so', and then another proposition, called the *conclusion*. This is best illustrated by an example:

If everything is determined, people are not free.	Premise
People are free.	Premise
So not everything is determined.	Conclusion

We will examine good arguments (like this one), in order to to give an account of why they are good.

One important way for an argument to be good is for the premises to guarantee the conclusion. That is, if the premises are true then the conclusion has to be true. Instead of simply calling arguments like this 'good' (which is not particularly helpful, as there are other ways arguments can be good), we will call them *valid*. So, to summarise:

> An argument is valid if and only if whenever the premises are true, so is the conclusion.
>
> In other words, it is impossible for the premises to be true while at the same time the conclusion is false.

It seems clear that our argument about determinism and freedom is valid. If the two premises are true, the conclusion invariably follows. If the conclusion is false – if not everything is determined – then one of the premises must be false. Either people are not free, or people can be free *despite* determinism.

This shows how valid arguments are important. They not only give us reasons to believe their conclusions – if you already believe the premises – they also exhibit connections between propositions that are important even if we do not believe the conclusions. If you believe everything is determined then you must reject one of the premises of our argument. The validity of the argument will not force you into one position or the other – it will instead help you to see what options are open to you.

There are *other* ways for arguments to be good. For example, consider the following argument.

> If people are mammals, they are not cold-blooded.
> People are cold-blooded.
> So people are not mammals.

This is clearly a valid argument, but no-one in their right mind would believe the conclusion. That's because the premises are false. (Well, the *second* premise is false – but that's enough. One premise being false is enough for the argument to be bad in this sense.) This gives us an idea for another definition:

> An argument is sound, just in the case where it is valid, and, in addition, the premises are all true. So, the conclusion of a sound argument must also be true.

Soundness appeals to more than mere validity. More than logical connections between premises and conclusion are required for an argument to be sound: soundness appeals also to the *truth* of the matter. The conclusion of a sound argument is always true. This is of course not the case for valid arguments. Some valid arguments have true conclusions and others have false conclusions.

Of course, if we disagree about the truth of the premises of an argument, this can lead to disagreement about the argument's soundness. If we have a valid argument for which we are uncertain about the truth of the premises, it follows that we ought to be uncertain about the soundness of the argument too.

There are yet more ways for arguments to be good or bad. One that we will not consider in this book is the issue of *inductive strength* or *weakness*. Sometimes we do not have enough information in our premises to *guarantee* the conclusion, but we might make the conclusion more likely than it might be otherwise. We say that an argument is inductively strong if, given the truth of the premises, the conclusion is likely. An argument is inductively weak if the truth of the premises does not make the conclusion *likely*. The study of inductive strength and weakness is the study of inductive logic. We will not explore inductive logic in this book. We will concentrate on what is called *deductive logic* – the study of *validity* of arguments.

Argument forms

Consider the two arguments we saw in the previous section. These arguments share something very important: their shape, or structure. We say the argument has the following *form*:

If *p* then not *q*
q
Therefore, not *p*

Both of our arguments have this form. The first argument has got exactly this shape. If we let *p* stand for 'everything is determined' and *q* stand for 'people are free' then we get the original argument back, more or less. I say 'more or less' because you must do a little fiddling to get the exact wording of the original argument. The fiddling is not hard, so I will not pause to examine it here.

The second argument has the same shape. In this case *p* stands for 'people are mammals' and *q* stands for the (less plausible) proposition 'people are cold-blooded'. This form of the argument is important, as any choice of propositions for *p* and *q* will make a valid argument. For example, when we choose 'utilitarianism is true' for *p* and 'we should always keep our promises' for *q*, we have this instance:

If utilitarianism is true, we should not always keep our promises.
We should always keep our promises.
So utilitarianism is not true.

Find other example arguments for yourself by choosing other propositions for *p* and *q*.

In general, a propositional form is found by replacing 'sub-propositions' inside a given proposition by letters. The result is said to be a *form* of the original proposition.

For example, 'If *p* then it will rain' is a form of 'If it is cloudy then it will rain', for we have replaced 'it is cloudy' by *p*. Similarly, 'If *p* then *q*' is a form of 'If it is cloudy then it will rain', as we have replaced *q* by 'it will rain'.

Given a propositional form, we say that a sentence is an *instance* of that form if we get the sentence (or a sentence with the same meaning) by replacing the single letters by sentences.

So, 'If it is cloudy then it will rain' is an instance of 'if *p* then *q*'. 'If Queensland bat first, they will score well' is also an instance of 'if *p* then *q*', where *p* is replaced by 'Queensland bat first' and *q* is replaced by 'Queensland will score well'. (It is better to choose this over 'they will score well', as this sentence will mean other things in different contexts.)

In propositional forms, we can repeat the same letter. For example 'maybe p and maybe not p' is a perfectly decent form, with instances 'maybe he will, and maybe he won't' and 'maybe Queensland will win, and maybe Queensland will not win'. In these cases, we must substitute the same sentence for each instance of the one letter. Finally, an argument form is made up of propositional forms as premises, and another propositional form as conclusion. An instance is found by replacing each instance of each letter by the one sentence.

When every instance of an argument form is valid, we call it a valid argument form, for the obvious reasons. If an argument is of a form that we know is valid then we know that the argument is valid. So, given a valid argument form, you can construct valid arguments to your heart's content. Valid arguments can be constructed out of valid argument forms, and formal logic is the study of argument forms. Our study of logic will concentrate on the study of forms of arguments.

Be warned – an argument can be an instance of an invalid form, while still being valid. As an example, our arguments are valid, but they *also* have the following form:

> If p then q
> r
> Therefore, s

which is *not* a valid form. This form has plenty of invalid instances. Here is one:

> If you are the Pope, you are Catholic.
> Two is an even number.
> Therefore, the moon is made of green cheese.

This argument is not valid, since the premises are true and the conclusion is false. However, this form has valid instances. Our original argument is given by letting p be 'everything is determined', q be 'people are not free', r be 'people are free' and s be 'not everything is determined'. This is a perfectly decent instance of our form. The argument is valid, but the form is not. This is not a problem for the idea of forms – it simply shows us that this new form is not descriptive or specific enough to account for the validity of the original argument. That argument is valid, but this second form is not specific enough to exhibit that validity. Our original form is specific enough.

Summary

So, to sum up, we have the following facts about validity and argument forms.

- For an argument to be *valid*, in any circumstance in which the premises are true, so is the conclusion.
- For an argument to be *invalid*, there has to be *some* possibility in which the premises are true and the conclusion is not true.
- An *argument form* exhibits some of the structure of an argument.
- If an argument has a particular form, that argument is said to be an *instance* of that argument form.
- An argument form is *valid* if and only if *every instance* of that form is valid.
- An instance of a valid argument form is *always* a valid argument.
- Instances of invalid forms *may* be valid.

Further reading

For much more on the difference between sentences that express propositions and those that do not, see A. C. Grayling's *An Introduction to Philosophical Logic*, Chapter 2 [8].

Mark Sainsbury's book *Logical Forms* is an introduction to logic that focuses on logical forms [25]. The exact boundary between logical form and non-logical form is a matter of a great deal of debate. Gila Sher's book *The Bounds of Logic* [26] is a technical discussion of the boundary between logical form and other notions of form that might not be appropriately called 'logical'.

Exercises

Each set of exercises is divided into two sections. Basic questions reinforce the ideas and concepts of the chapter. Advanced questions extend the material to other areas, and are harder. Attempt each basic question, until you have mastered the material. Then go on to the advanced questions.

Basic

{1.1} Which of these sentences express propositions? What do the other sentences express? (Examples might be *questions, commands, exclamations, wishes.*)

1 Sydney is north of Melbourne.
2 Is Edinburgh in Scotland?
3 The moon is made of swiss cheese.
4 Did you see the eclipse?
5 What an eclipse!
6 Would that I were good at logic.
7 Look at the eclipse.
8 I wish that I were good at logic.
9 $7 + 12 = 23$
10 If you get Kelly you will be rewarded.

{1.2} Consider the following argument forms:

Modus Ponens
If p then q
p
Therefore q

Modus Tollens
If p then q
not q
Therefore not p

Hypothetical Syllogism
If p then q
If q then r
Therefore if p then r

Affirming the Consequent
If p then q
q
Therefore p

17

Disjunctive Syllogism	*Disjunction Introduction*
Either p or q	If p then r
Not p	If q then r
Therefore q	Therefore if either p or q then r

In these argument forms, instances are found by substituting propositions for p, q and r. Which of these argument forms are valid? Of the forms that are invalid, find instances that are not valid, and instances that are valid.

{1.3} Consider the following arguments:

1   Greg and Caroline teach *PHIL137*.
     Caroline teaches Critical Thinking and *PHIL132*.
     Therefore Greg teaches *PHIL137* and Caroline teaches *PHIL132*.
2   Greg and Caroline teach *PHIL137*.
     Caroline and Catriona teach *PHIL132*.
     Therefore Greg teaches *PHIL137* but not *PHIL132*.
3   Greg teaches *PHIL137* and *PHIL280*.
     Caroline teaches *PHIL137*.
     Therefore Greg and Caroline teach *PHIL137*.

For each argument, which of the following forms does it exhibit?

1   p and q, r and s; therefore t
2   p, q; therefore r
3   p and q, q and r; therefore p and r

Advanced

{1.4} It is not always easy to tell whether or not a sentence expresses a proposition. What do you think of these?

1   2 + the Pacific Ocean = Beethoven
2   The present King of France is bald.[1]
3   This sentence is false.
4   This sentence is true.

5 'Twas brillig, and the slithy toves did gyre and gimble in the wabe.'

Do they express propositions? If so, are they true, or are they false? Or are they something else? Opinions diverge on strange cases like these – what do you think?

{1.5} Does every invalid argument form have valid instances?

{1.6} Does every valid argument possess a valid form?

> It is undesirable to believe a proposition
> when there is no ground whatever
> for supposing it true.
> – Bertrand Russell

Note

1   France has no king at present.

Chapter 2

Connectives and argument forms

As you saw in the last chapter, arguments have different forms, and we can use forms of arguments in our study of validity and invalidity of arguments. The forms of an argument bring to light a kind of *structure* exhibited by the argument. Different sorts of forms expose different sorts of structure. The first kind of structure we will examine is the structure given by *propositional connectives*. These connectives give us ways to construct new propositions out of old propositions. The connectives form the 'nuts and bolts' in many different argument forms. The resulting theory is called *propositional logic* and it will be the focus of the first half of this book.

Conjunction and disjunction

Consider the two propositions

> An action is good when it makes people happy.
> Keeping your promises is always good.

You might believe both of these propositions. You can assert both in one go by asserting their conjunction:

An action is good when it makes people happy,
and keeping your promises is always good.

This is a *single* proposition – you may believe it or reject it, or simply be undecided. It is a special proposition, because it is related to two other propositions. It is said to be the *conjunction* of the original propositions. The conjunction is true just when both conjuncts are true. If either of the original propositions is false, the conjunction is false.

More generally, given two propositions p and q, their *conjunction* is the proposition

$$p \mathbin{\&} q$$

The original propositions p and q are the said to be the *conjuncts* of $p \mathbin{\&} q$. We use the ampersand symbol '&' as a handy shorthand for 'and' when describing forms of propositions.

Sometimes a sentence uses the word 'and' to connect parts of speech other than phrases. For example the 'and' in the sentence

Justice and tolerance are valuable.

connects the words justice and tolerance, and these words do not (by themselves) express propositions. However, the sentence is *still* a kind of conjunction. At the very least, it seems to have the same meaning as the conjunction of the two sentences

Justice is valuable.   Tolerance is valuable.

because saying Justice and tolerance are valuable is a shorter way of saying the more long winded Justice is valuable and tolerance is valuable.

However, you must be careful! Sometimes sentences feature the word 'and', *without* expressing conjunctions of propositions. For example, sometimes an 'and' does not join different propositions, but it joins something else. For example, if I say

21

> Colleen and Errol got married.

this is *not* a conjunction of two propositions. It certainly is not the conjunction of the propositions **Colleen got married** and **Errol got married**, since that proposition

> Colleen got married and Errol got married.

means something else. That conjunction does not say that Colleen and Errol married each other, whereas (at least in the colloquial speech familiar to me) to say **Colleen and Errol got married** is to say that they *did* marry each other.

Furthermore, sometimes we use 'and' to join two propositions and it still does not express a simple conjunction. Sometimes we use 'and' to indicate a kind of order between the two propositions. For example, the two sentences

> I went out and had dinner.   I had dinner and went out.

say very different things. The first indicates that you went out and *then* had dinner. The second indicates that you had dinner and *then* went out. These are not propositional conjunctions in our sense, because making sure that 'I had dinner' and that 'I went out' are true is not enough to make it true that 'I went out and had dinner'. For that, we require the right kind of order.

For one last example of an 'and' that is not a conjunction, consider this case: a woman points a gun at you, and says

> One false move and I shoot.

She is saying that *if* you make a false move, she will shoot. The conjunction of the two propositions, on the other hand, asserts *that* you will make one false move, *and* that she will shoot. This is obviously a different claim (and a different threat).

It is a matter of some art to determine which 'and' claims really are conjunctions and which are not. We will not pursue this point here. Instead, we will look at other ways to combine propositions to form new ones.

We can assert that (at least) one of a pair of propositions is true by asserting their disjunction. For example, in the case of the good being what makes people happy, and the goodness of keeping your promises, you might think that keeping your promises is probably a good thing. But you've been reading the work of some utilitarians who make it seem pretty plausible to you that the good is grounded in human happiness. You're undecided about the merits of utilitarianism, but you can at least claim this disjunction:

> Either an action is good when it makes people happy,
> or keeping your promises is always good.

because you think that keeping promises is mostly good, and the only way that it could be bad is in those cases where keeping a promise prevents human happiness.

Given two propositions p and q, we write their *disjunction* as '$p \vee q$'. The original propositions p and q are said to be the *disjuncts* of $p \vee q$. The disjunction $p \vee q$ is true just when either of the disjuncts is true.

Disjunctions can be *inclusive* or *exclusive*. An inclusive disjunction leaves open the possibility that both disjuncts are true, while an exclusive disjunction rules out this possibility. The difference can be made explicit like this:

> Either an action is good when it makes people happy,
> or keeping your promises is always good (and possibly both).

This is inclusive. You assert this when you think that utilitarianism might rule out the goodness of keeping promises, but it might not. Perhaps keeping promises does, on the whole, make people happier than they would otherwise be.

If you think this is not a possibility then you can assert the *exclusive* disjunction:

> Either an action is good when it makes people happy,
> or keeping your promises is always good (and not both).

In our study of connectives, we will use inclusive disjunction more than exclusive disjunction, so we will read '$p \vee q$' as the inclusive disjunction of the propositions *p* and *q*. (The symbol '∨' comes from the Latin *vel* for 'or'.)

Conditionals and biconditionals

Conjunctions combine pairs of propositions by asserting that *both* are true, and disjunctions combine them by asserting that *at least one* is true. Another way to combine propositions is to assert *connections* between them. For example, in your study of utilitarianism, you might conclude not that utilitarianism is true, or that it is false (you're not convinced of either side here), but you are convinced that:

> If an action is good when it makes people happy
> then keeping your promises is always good.

More generally, given two propositions *p* and *q*, I can assert the conditional proposition 'if *p* then *q*'. The original proposition *p* is the *antecedent*, and *q* is the *consequent* of the conditional. We give the two parts different names because they perform different functions in the complex proposition. The proposition 'if *p* then *q*' is very different from the proposition 'if *q* then *p*'.

With conditionals, you have to watch out. The following all assert *the same kind* of connection between *p* and *q*, despite the different phrasing and ordering:

$$\text{If } p \text{ then } q \quad \text{If } p, q \quad q \text{ if } p \quad p \text{ only if } q$$

In each of these forms of sentences, *p* is the antecedent and *q* is the consequent. Here is a technique for remembering this fact: 'If *p*' signals that *p* is the *antecedent* of a conditional, whether it occurs at the beginning or the end of a sentence. So, 'if *p* then *q*' and '*q*, if *p*' assert the same kind of connection between *p* and *q*. They both say that under the conditions that *p* occurs, so does *q*. On the other hand, '*only if q*' signals that *q* is the *consequent*. If *p* is true *only* if *q* is true, then if *p* is true, so is *q*.

Think of examples. If you know that if *p* then *q*, then once you find out that *p* is true, you know that *q* is true too. 'Only if' is the other way around. If you know that p only if q, then finding out that p still tells you that q is true too. So 'p only if q' has the same effect as 'if p then q'.

This does not mean that the forms 'if p then q' and 'p only if q' have exactly the same significance in all circumstances. If I say 'p only if q', I might signal that q is some kind of *condition* for p. For example, when I say

> I go to the beach only if it is fine.

I am saying that fine weather is a condition for going to the beach. It sounds a little more surprising to say

> If I go to the beach, it is fine.

for in this case it sounds as if I am saying that my going to the beach *makes* it fine. It sounds as if the relation of dependence goes in the other direction. However, in each case, I go to the beach is the antecedent, and it is fine is the consequent, for in either case, if I am at the beach, it follows that it is fine.

Whatever words we use to express conditionals, we will write a conditional statement with antecedent p and consequent q as

$$p \supset q$$

The antecedent is the condition under which the outcome (the consequent) occurs.

We can indicate that a two-way connection holds between propositions by asserting a *biconditional* statement:

> An action is good when it makes people happy if and only if keeping your promises is always good.

Given two propositions p and q, the proposition p if and only if q is their *biconditional*. We call p and q its *left-hand* and *right-hand expressions* respectively. For symbolism, we write the biconditional as

$$p \equiv q$$

Note that the biconditional $p \equiv q$ has the same meaning as $(p \supset q)$ & $(q \supset p)$, the conjunction of the two conditionals $p \supset q$ and $q \supset p$.

In written English, you can abbreviate 'if and only if' by the shorter 'iff'. This is still read aloud as 'if and only if'. I will use this abbreviation in the rest of the book.

Negation

One last way to form new propositions from old is provided by *negation*. We can assert the negation of a proposition simply by using a judiciously placed 'not'. Here is an example:

> Keeping your promises is not always good.

This is the negation of

> Keeping your promises is always good.

You have to be careful in where you place the 'not' in a proposition in order to negate it. What we want is a proposition that simply states that the original proposition is false. We get a different proposition if we place the 'not' somewhere else. If I say

> Keeping your promises is always not good.

I say something much stronger than the original negation. I'm saying that keeping promises is always bad – it is *never* good. This goes much further than simply denying the claim that keeping your promises is always a good thing.

In general, given a proposition p, you can express the negation of p by saying 'it's not the case that p'. This is cumbersome, but it works in every case. We say that this proposition is the negation of p, and the original proposition p is the *negand* of the negation. We write the negation of p as

$$\sim p$$

Strictly speaking, negation is not a *connective*, as it does not connect different propositions. It is an operator, as it operates on the original proposition to provide another. However, we will abuse the terminology just a little, and call each of conjunction, disjunction, negation, the conditional and the biconditional connectives.

There are many more connectives that can be used to build propositions from others. Examples are 'I believe that . . .', 'Max hopes that . . .', 'It is possible that . . .', '. . . because . . .', and many many more. We will concentrate on the connectives already seen, for they form the core of a lot of our reasoning, and they are, by far, the simplest connectives to deal with. In Chapter 6 we will look a little at operators for possibility and necessity, but for now we focus on the connectives we have already considered: conjunction, disjunction, the conditional and biconditional, and negation.

A Language of forms

To summarise what we have seen so far, we have symbols for each of the propositional connectives (Table 2.1). We can use these connectives to form the basis for a formal language, a language of forms, to describe the structure of arguments. We use a basic stock of symbols to represent propositions. There is nothing special about the particular symbols we use, as long as we have enough of them, and as long as we don't use any of the connectives as symbols standing for propositions (that would be too confusing). We will always use lower-case letters, and if that isn't enough, we

Table 2.1 **Propositional connectives**

Name	Reading	Symbol
Conjunction	. . . and . . .	&
Disjunction	. . . or . . .	∨
Conditional	if . . . then . . .	⊃
Biconditional	. . . if and only if . . .	≡
Negation	not	~

will resort to lower-case letters subscripted by numbers. So, here are some examples:

$$p \quad q \quad j \quad k \quad r_3 \quad s_{14}$$

These symbols are called *atomic propositions*, or *atomic formulas*, because they have no significant parts. (As far as we are concerned, p_{14} has nothing more to do with p_{15} than it has to do with q. Each atomic proposition is unrelated to all others.) They are *atoms*.

We then use the connectives to form new propositions from old, using a number of rules. The rules go like this:

- Any atomic formula is a formula.
- If A is a formula, so is $\sim A$.
- If A and B are formulas, so are $(A \& B)$, $(A \lor B)$, $(A \supset B)$ and $(A \equiv B)$.
- Nothing else is a formula.

So, things like

$$((p \& q) \supset r) \quad \sim\sim((p \lor \sim q) \equiv \sim r) \quad (((p \supset q) \& (q \supset r)) \lor (p \supset r))$$

are all formulas, as they are built up from the atomic formulas by way of the rules. For example:

- p and q are formulas (they are atoms).
- So, $(p \& q)$ is a formula (it is a conjunction of the two formulas p and q).
- r is a formula (it is an atom).
- So, $((p \& q) \supset r)$ is a formula (it is a conditional made up of two formulas: $(p \& q)$ and r).

The other two example formulas are built up using the rules in a similar way. We sometimes call these formulas *well formed* to contrast with collections of symbols that are not formulas.

The following expressions are built from the atomic formulas using the connectives and negation, but they are not formulas, because they cannot be built up using the formation rules:

$$p\sim \quad (p \,\&\, q \,\&\, r) \quad \equiv pq \quad (p \equiv q \supset \sim r)$$

The first, $p\sim$, is not a formula, since a negation always attaches to a formula on its left. The second, $(p \,\&\, q \,\&\, r)$, is not a formula, since the rule for introducing conjunctions always wraps parentheses around the conjuncts. To form a three-place conjunction, you must use either $(p \,\&\, (q \,\&\, r))$ or $((p \,\&\, q) \,\&\, r)$.

The case of the other two non-formulas is similar. The biconditional should be used *between* other formulas, not *prefixing* them, and in the last example, we should either bracket $(p \equiv q)$ or $(q \supset \sim r)$.

We say that a formula is *complex* if and only if it is not atomic. Complex formulas always involve connectives, and we say that the *main connective* of a complex formula is the connective that was last added in its construction. An atomic formula has no main connective, since it contains no connectives at all.

The main connectives of each of the formulas displayed above are given in Table 2.2.

Finally, to save us from writing too many pairs of parentheses, we will ignore the outermost set of parentheses in any formula, if the main connective is not a negation. So, we write

$$(p \,\&\, q) \supset r \quad \text{instead of} \quad ((p \,\&\, q) \supset r)$$

That completes the definition of formulas. We will use formulas to define argument forms, and to study them.

Table 2.2 **Main connectives of displayed formulas**

Formula	Main connective
$((p \,\&\, q) \supset r)$	$\supset$
$\sim\sim((p \vee \sim q) \equiv \sim r)$	$\sim$
$(((p \supset q) \,\&\, (q \supset r)) \vee (p \supset r))$	$\vee$

More argument forms

We have just considered different forms of propositions made out of other propositions. These are called *complex* propositions. And a proposition that is not complex is said to be *atomic*. Given an argument, we can find its *most descriptive* propositional argument form by analysing the structure of its propositions. We do this by forming a *dictionary* of the atomic propositions in the argument, and rewriting the argument in terms of these atomic propositions. An example will illustrate the process. Take the argument:

> If the dog ran away, the gate was open.
> If the gate was open, Anne didn't close it.
> Therefore, if Anne closed the gate, the dog did not run away.

The atomic propositions in this argument are

> The dog ran away.   The gate was open.   Anne closed the gate.

All the propositions in the argument are made out of these atomic propositions using our connectives. So, we let atomic formulas stand for these propositions. We can make a dictionary to record the letters standing for each proposition:

$$r = \text{The dog ran away}$$
$$o = \text{The gate was open}$$
$$c = \text{Anne closed the gate}$$

Then we have the following argument form:

$$r \supset o$$
$$o \supset {\sim}c$$
$$\text{Therefore, } c \supset {\sim}r$$

This *argument form* exhibits the shape of the original argument. Let's do another example. We will find the most descriptive form of this argument:

If you're going to the party, Max won't come.
If Max comes to the party, I'll have a good time if Julie's there too.
Therefore, if you're going to the party but Julie's not, I won't have a good time.

We formulate the dictionary of atomic propositions, choosing letters as appropriate:

$$p = \text{You're going to the party}$$
$$m = \text{Max comes to the party}$$
$$g = \text{I'll have a good time}$$
$$j = \text{Julie is at the party}$$

We then have the following form:

$$p \supset {\sim}m$$
$$m \supset (j \supset g)$$
$$\text{Therefore, } (p \mathbin{\&} {\sim}j) \supset {\sim}g$$

This example is more difficult. We had to 'massage' the atomic propositions to make the dictionary. For example, j is Julie is at the party not Julie's there too. Second, we have read the 'but' in the conclusion as a conjunction. We formalise you're going to the party but Julie's not as $p \mathbin{\&} {\sim}j$; literally, you are going to the party and it is not the case that Julie is at the party. Despite all these changes, we have not done too much violence to the original argument to read it in this way.[1] Once we have argument forms, we use the techniques of formal logic to study the forms.

There is much more that can be said about finding forms of arguments. However, we will go on to actually analyse argument forms in the next chapter. To get more experience in discerning forms, go through the exercises.

Summary

Here is the formal language we have defined:

- We have a stock of *atomic* formulas, written using lower-case letters.

- If A and B are formulas, their *conjunction* $(A \And B)$ is a formula. $(A \And B)$ is read 'A and B'.
- If A and B are formulas, their *disjunction* $(A \lor B)$ is a formula. $(A \lor B)$ is read 'A or B'. Disjunctions may be inclusive (A or B or both) or exclusive (A or B but not both).
- If A and B are formulas, their *conditional* $(A \supset B)$ is a formula. $(A \supset B)$ is read 'if A then B'. A is the *antecedent* and B is the *consequent* of the conditional.
- If A and B are formulas, their *biconditional* $(A \equiv B)$ is a formula. $(A \equiv B)$ is read 'A if and only if B', and 'if and only if' is often abbreviated as 'iff'.
- If A is a formula, then its *negation* $\sim A$ is also a formula. $\sim A$ is read 'it is not the case that A', or simply 'not A'.
- A *atomic* proposition is a proposition that is not a conjunction, disjunction, conditional, biconditional or negation.
- You can find the *most descriptive propositional form* of an argument by forming a *dictionary* of the atomic propositions in the argument, and then rewriting the argument in terms of these atomic propositions, replacing each atomic proposition in the argument by an atomic formula.

Exercises

{2.1} For each of the following negations, find its *negand*:

1 Greg is not in town.
2 Fred is not very smart.
3 Minh isn't a bad student.
4 Not every car is fuel-efficient.
5 That car is neither red nor a diesel.

{2.2} For each of the following conjunctions, find both *conjuncts*:

1 It is −5 degrees and the clouds are grey.
2 He was tired but he wanted to keep going.
3 Although the waves were breaking, the surf was low.
4 In spite of there being a strike, the power was not cut.
5 Fred and Jack are not mechanics.

{2.3} For each of the following disjunctions, find both *disjuncts*:

1   Either Eric is there or Yukiko is there.
2   The car is either white or yellow.
3   Brian is doing a Ph.D. or a Masters degree.
4   Either it rains or it doesn't.
5   I'll have coffee or tea.

{2.4} For each of the following conditionals, find the *antecedent* and the *consequent*:

1   If it is raining, I'll walk home.
2   If you look outside, you'll see the nice garden I planted.
3   If I'm tired, I don't do my logic very well.
4   I do logic well only if I'm awake.
5   I do logic well if I'm awake.
6   You will pass if you work hard.
7   The world's future is assured only if we get rid of nuclear weapons.
8   The world's future is assured if we get rid of nuclear weapons.
9   If Oswald didn't shoot Kennedy, someone else did.
10 If Oswald hadn't shot Kennedy, someone else would have.

{2.5} For each of the following complex propositions, determine what kind of proposition it is, and the sub-propositions that went into its construction. If these propositions are complex, continue the process until you get to atomic propositions. (For example, for the proposition *Max is a PHIL134 student and he isn't doing badly*, we analyse it like this: It is a conjunction, with conjuncts *Max is a PHIL134 student* and *Max is not doing badly*. *Max is a PHIL134 student* is atomic. *Max is not doing badly* is a negation, with the negand *Max is doing badly*.)

1   Christine is happy if she is not thinking about her thesis.
2   I don't know if she's coming to the party.
3   If Theodore is enrolled in PHIL134, and he passes, he can go on to do advanced logic subjects.

4   If Theodore isn't enrolled in PHIL134, or if he doesn't pass, then he cannot go on to do advanced logic subjects.

5   I believe, and you know, that you are either going to leave the party early or make a scene.

{2.6} Use the dictionary

$$y = \text{Yukiko is a linguist}$$
$$c = \text{Christine is a lawyer}$$
$$p = \text{Pavlos is a logician}$$

and translate the following formulas:

1   $\sim y$
2   $\sim y \lor p$
3   $\sim y \equiv c$
4   $y \supset (c \supset p)$
5   $(y \mathbin{\&} \sim p) \supset c$
6   $y \mathbin{\&} c$
7   $\sim(y \mathbin{\&} p)$
8   $\sim(y \equiv c)$
9   $\sim\sim c$
10 $y \equiv (c \lor \sim p)$
11 $y \lor c$
12 $y \equiv p$
13 $y \supset c$
14 $y \supset (c \supset p)$
15 $(y \supset c) \equiv (c \supset y)$

{2.7} Translate the following sentences into formulas (using the same dictionary):

1   Christine is not a lawyer.
2   Yukiko is a linguist and Pavlos is a logician.
3   If Pavlos is a logician then Yukiko is a linguist.
4   Either Pavlos is a logician or Yukiko is not a linguist.
5   It's not the case that both Pavlos is a logician and Christine is a lawyer.
6   Yukiko is a linguist only if both Pavlos is a logician and Christine is not a lawyer.

7 Christine is a lawyer if either Yukiko is a linguist or Pavlos is not a logician.

8 Yukiko is a linguist if and only if either Pavlos is a logician or Christine is not a lawyer.

9 Either Pavlos is a logician, or Yukiko is a linguist only if Christine is a lawyer.

10 Either Pavlos is a logician or Yukiko is a linguist, only if Christine is a lawyer.

{2.8} Which of the following are well-formed formulas?

1 $\sim p$
2 $p\sim\sim$
3 $(p \mathbin{\&} \sim q) \supset (\sim q \mathbin{\&} q$
4 $\sim q \supset (p \supset \sim p)$
5 $p \vee q \vee r$
6 $\sim\sim r$
7 $p \supset q \supset r$
8 $(p \supset q) \equiv q \equiv r$
9 $\sim p \mathbin{\&} q$
10 $p \mathbin{\&} \sim p$

> I am not a crook.
> – Richard Nixon

Note

1 If there is any more information in you're going to the party but Julie's not over and above you are going to the party and it is not the case that Julie is at the party, it is probably to be found in our expectations of this conjunction being *surprising*, and not in any more facts about who is at the party and what might happen.

Chapter 3

Truth tables

In the last chapter, we introduced a formal language, to describe the structure of arguments. We will now use this formal language to analyse argument forms. To do this, we will examine how each connective interacts with truth and falsity, since the truth and falsity of the premises and conclusions of arguments are involved so intimately with the validity of arguments.

Truth tables

We can now go some way in finding how the connectives work in arguments, by noting that propositions are the sort of things that can be true, or false. And the truth value of a complex proposition depends crucially on the truth value of the propositions out of which it is made.

To take a simple example, if p is true then its negation, $\sim p$ is false. And if p is false then $\sim p$ is true. Writing this in a table, with 1 to stand for true and 0 for false, we get this table:

p	$\sim p$
0	1
1	0

In this table, the two rows represent the two different possibilities for the truth of p. In the first row (or the first *case* as we will sometimes say), p is false. In that case, $\sim p$ is true. In the second row, p is true, so in that case, $\sim p$ is false.

Negation is simplest, as it is a one-place connective. The other connectives have two places, as they combine two propositions. Given two propositions, p and q, there are four different cases of truth and falsity:

p	q
0	0
0	1
1	0
1	1

If p is false, there are two possibilities for q. On the other hand, if p is true, there are two possibilities for q. That makes $2 \times 2 = 4$. (Similarly, given three propositions, p, q and r, there are eight different possibilities, since there are the four for p and q, combined with r being true, and the same four, combined with r being false. More generally, given n different propositions, there are $2 \times 2 \times \cdots \times 2$ (n times), which is 2^n different cases.)

Anyway, back to the other connectives. Let's start with conjunction. The conjunction $p \,\&\, q$ is true just when p and q are both true, and it is false otherwise. So, the table for conjunction goes like this:

p	q	$p \,\&\, q$
0	0	0
0	1	0
1	0	0
1	1	1

The only row in which the conjunction p & q is true is the row in which both p and q are true. In all other rows, the conjunction is false.

The disjunction, $p \vee q$, is true just when at least one of p and q are true. Recall that we treat disjunction as inclusive. If both disjuncts are true then the whole disjunction is true. If just one disjunction is true then the whole disjunction is true. So, we have this table:

p	q	$p \vee q$
0	0	0
0	1	1
1	0	1
1	1	1

The only row in which the disjunction is false is the row in which both disjuncts are false.

Before going on to consider the other connectives, let's see how we can use truth tables to deal with more complex propositions. Let's consider the formula $\sim(p$ & $\sim q)$. This is the negation of the conjunction p & $\sim q$, which is the conjunction of the atomic formula p with the negation $\sim q$. The truth value of this formula depends on the values of p and q, so there are four different cases to consider. We start with a table like this, which displays the atomic formulas to the left, to indicate the four different cases.

p	q	$\sim$	(p	&	$\sim$	q)
0	0					
0	1					
1	0					
1	1					

To calculate this truth value of the complex proposition, we first must calculate the value of $\sim q$ in terms of the value of q. So, we repeat the values of q under where it occurs here, and then we write the values of $\sim q$ *under the negation sign*, which is the main connective of the negation ~q. This gives us the next stage of the production of the table:

p	q	~	(p	&	~	q)
0	0				1	0
0	1				0	1
1	0				1	0
1	1				0	1

Now, equipped with the values of ~q in each case, we can calculate the value of the conjunction p & ~q in each case. We repeat the value of p under the 'p' occurring in the proposition, and then we use this value together with the value of ~q, to find the value of the conjunction, using the table for the conjunction. We write the value of the conjunction, in each case, under the ampersand. This gives us the following table:

p	q	~	(p	&	~	q)
0	0		0	0	1	0
0	1		0	0	0	1
1	0		1	1	1	0
1	1		1	0	0	1

The third row is the only case in which p and ~q are both true, so it is the only case in which the conjunction p & ~q is true. To complete the table, we negate the value of p & ~q and write the result under the negation sign, the main connective of the whole formula:

p	q	~	(p	&	~	q)
0	0	1	0	0	1	0
0	1	1	0	0	0	1
1	0	0	1	1	1	0
1	1	1	1	0	0	1

We have written this in boldface to indicate that this column provides the value of the whole proposition in each different case. This technique can be generalised to provide the truth values of formulas as complex as you please. For formulas containing three different atomic formulas, we have a table of eight rows, for formulas containing four atomic formulas, we have sixteen rows, and so on. Each row of the table represents a different *possibility* or *case*. No matter what truth value had by the atomic propositions p, q, r and so on, the corresponding row of the truth table tells you the truth value of the complex formula made up of those atomic formulas.

Now, to complete our definition of truth tables for complex formulas, we need to see the tables for the conditional and the biconditional. These cases are a little more involved than those for the other connectives.

The conditional $p \supset q$ has the same truth table as the complex proposition $\sim(p \;\&\; \sim q)$. We have already seen this table. This proposition is false only when p is true and q is false, and it is true in each other case.

p	q	$p \supset q$
0	0	1
0	1	1
1	0	0
1	1	1

The conditional $p \supset q$ has this truth table because the conditional is intimately connected to $\sim(p \;\&\; \sim q)$. Consider the two following lines of reasoning.

- If $p \supset q$ is true then if p is true, q must be true (that is what a conditional says, after all), so you do not have p true and q false, so $p \;\&\; \sim q$ is not true, and consequently, $\sim(p \;\&\; \sim q)$ is true.
- Conversely, if $\sim(p \;\&\; \sim q)$ is true, consider what happens if p is true. In that case, you don't have q false, since $p \;\&\; \sim q$ is not true (that is what we have assumed: $\sim(p \;\&\; \sim q)$ is true). So, if you don't have q false, q must be true. So if p is true, so is q. In other words, $p \supset q$ is true.

According to these two small arguments $p \supset q$ has the same truth value as $\sim(p \mathbin{\&} \sim q)$, and so $p \supset q$ is false only when p is true and q is false. A conditional is false if and only if there is an explicit counterexample – that is, if and only if the antecedent is true, and the consequent is false.

In Chapter 6, we will discuss the interpretation of the conditional further, as not everyone is happy with this analysis. For now, however, we will use this truth table for the conditional. The conditional defined in this way is *often* called the material conditional, to make clear that alternate definitions for the conditional are possible.

The only remaining connective is the *biconditional*. The biconditional $p \equiv q$ acts like the conjunction of $p \supset q$ and $q \supset p$. As a result, it is false if p is true and q is false, or if p is false and q is true. It is true otherwise. So, it has this table:

p	q	$p \equiv q$
0	0	1
0	1	0
1	0	0
1	1	1

In this table, $p \equiv q$ is true if and only if p and q have the same truth value.

Before going on to see how we can use truth tables to evaluate argument forms, let's see another example of a truth table for a complex proposition, this time for $((p \equiv q) \mathbin{\&} p) \supset q$:

p	q	$((p$	$\equiv$	$q)$	$\&$	$p)$	$\supset$	q
0	0	0	1	0	0	0	1	0
0	1	0	0	1	0	0	1	1
1	0	1	0	0	0	1	1	0
1	1	1	1	1	1	1	1	1

We have used exactly the same technique to construct this table. First we find the values for $p \equiv q$, given the values of p and q. Then we can find the values of the conjunction $(p \equiv q) \mathbin{\&} p$. Finally, we combine this value with that of q, to get the truth value of the entire proposition, in each row. This is the column in boldface.

You will notice that this proposition is special. No matter what values p and q have, the proposition $((p \equiv q) \& p) \supset q$ is always true. We call such a proposition a *tautology*. Now matter how things are, a tautology is true.

We call a proposition that is false in every row a *contradiction*, or we will call it *inconsistent*. Here is an example contradiction with its truth table:

p	q	$((p$	$\supset$	$q)$	$\&$	$p)$	$\&$	$\sim$	q
0	0	0	1	0	0	0	0	1	0
0	1	0	1	1	0	0	0	0	1
1	0	1	0	0	0	1	0	1	0
1	1	1	1	1	1	1	0	0	1

If a proposition is neither a tautology nor a contradiction, there are some cases in which it is true and some cases in which it is false. These are called *contingent* propositions.

The general method for making truth tables for propositions is given in Box 3.1.

Each row of the truth table represents a *way the world could be*. To make sure we represent all possible circumstances, we distribute every possible combination of truth values (true and false) to each atomic proposition. Then the values of more complex propositions are built up from the values of simpler propositions. If a proposition has the value 'true' no matter what the value of the atomic propositions then it must be true, no matter what the world is like. It is a tautology. Conversely, if it cannot be true, it is a contradiction. If it could be true, and it could be false, it is a contingency.

In the rest of this book, we will call each row of a truth table an *evaluation* of the formulas. We say that an evaluation *satisfies* a formula when the formula is assigned the value 1. It follows that tautologies are satisfied in every evaluation, contradictions are satisfied in no evaluation, and contingencies are sometimes satisfied and sometimes not.

Box 3.1   Construction of truth tables for propositions

- Write the proposition in question, and list its atomic propositions to one side.
- Draw enough rows (2^n for n atomic propositions) and put the different combinations of 0s and 1s under the atomic propositions.
- Repeat these columns under the atomic propositions in the formula.
- Then work *outwards* using the rules.
- The column containing the main connective gives the value of the formula. This is the *final* column.
- If the final column contains no zeros, then the proposition is always true, it is a *tautology*.
- If the final column contains no ones, the proposition is never true, and it is is a *contradiction*, it is *inconsistent*.
- If it is neither of these, it is sometimes true and sometimes false, and then it is said to be *contingent*.

Truth tables for arguments

You also can use truth tables and evaluations to examine argument forms. To do this, you make one table evaluating the premises and the conclusion of the argument. This will give you a list of all of the different possibilities pertaining to the premises and the conclusion, and you will be able to use this to check if there is any possibility in which the premises are true and the conclusion is false.

Here is an evaluation of the argument form $p \supset q$, $q \supset p$, therefore $p \equiv q$:

p	q	p	$\supset$	q	q	$\supset$	p	p	$\equiv$	q
0	0	0	1	0	0	1	0	0	1	0
0	1	0	1	1	1	0	0	0	0	1
1	0	1	0	0	0	1	1	1	0	0
1	1	1	1	1	1	1	1	1	1	1

In this case, the argument form is *valid*, since the only cases in which the premises are both true (shown here in the first and the fourth rows) are cases in which the conclusion is also true. Using the technical terminology of the previous section, any evaluation that satisfies both of the premises also satisfies the conclusion. We symbolise this as follows:

$$p \supset q, q \supset p \models p \equiv q$$

The symbol '$\models$' records the validity of the argument form. We say that the premises entail the conclusion.

If X is a set of formulas and A is a formula then X entails A (written '$X \models A$') if and only if every evaluation satisfying every formula in X also satisfies A. Or, equivalently, there is no evaluation that satisfies X that does not also satisfy A.

Truth tables also give us the tools for exhibiting the invalidity of argument forms. Consider the argument form that proceeds from the premises $p \supset q$ and $\sim p$ to the conclusion $\sim q$. The table looks like this:

p	q	p	$\supset$	q	$\sim$	p	$\sim$	q
0	0	0	1	0	1	0	1	0
0	1	0	1	1	1	0	0	1
1	0	1	0	0	0	1	1	0
1	1	1	1	1	0	1	0	1

In this table, we do have a case in which the premises are true and the conclusion false. The second row provides an evaluation that satisfies both premises, but fails to satisfy the conclusion. We register the invalidity of the argument form with a slashed '$\models$'. We write

$$p \supset q, \sim p \not\models \sim q$$

to say that the premises do not entail the conclusion. The truth table gives us more information than the mere invalidity of the argument. It also provides an evaluation in which the premises are true and the conclusion false. The second row is such an evaluation. We write the evaluation like this:

$$p = 0 \quad q = 1$$

This evaluation is a counterexample to the argument form. It gives us a way to make the premises true and the conclusion false.

Let us consider a longer example. We will show that

$$\sim p \vee (q \supset r), \sim q \supset r \vDash p \supset r$$

In other words, we will show that the argument form from $\sim p \vee (q \supset r)$ and $\sim q \supset r$ to $p \supset r$ is valid. The table has eight rows, as the argument form has three atomic formulas:

p	q	r	~	p	v	(q	⊃	r)	~	q	⊃	r	p	⊃	r
0	0	0	1	0	1	0	1	0	1	0	0	0	0	1	0
0	0	1	1	0	1	0	1	1	1	0	1	1	0	1	1
0	1	0	1	0	1	1	0	0	0	1	1	0	0	1	0
0	1	1	1	0	1	1	1	1	0	1	1	1	0	1	1
1	0	0	0	1	1	0	1	0	1	0	0	0	1	0	0
1	0	1	0	1	1	0	1	1	1	0	1	1	1	1	1
1	1	0	0	1	0	1	0	0	0	1	1	0	1	0	0
1	1	1	0	1	1	1	1	1	0	1	1	1	1	1	1

The table has two rows in which the conclusion is false: rows 5 and 7. In row 5, the second premise is false, and in row 7, the first premise is false, so there is no evaluation satisfying both premises that does not also satisfy the conclusion.

Before we depart truth tables, it is interesting to note that tables give us a *decision procedure* for the valid argument forms in the propositional calculus. Given any (finite) argument form, we can find in a finite (but perhaps very long) time whether or not it is valid. Not every system of rules for determining validity has this property.

Finding evaluations quickly

For all the good things about truth tables, it is obvious that making the truth tables of big formulas or for long arguments takes up a lot of time and space. Try this one, for example:

$$((((((p_1 \supset p_2) \mathrel{\&} (p_2 \supset p_3)) \mathrel{\&} (p_3 \supset p_4)) \mathrel{\&} (p_4 \supset p_5) \mathrel{\&}$$
$$(p_5 \supset p_6)) \mathrel{\&} (p_6 \supset p_7)) \mathrel{\&} (p_7 \supset p_8)) \supset (p_1 \supset p_8)$$

It would take $2^8 = 256$ rows, which is a lot more than I am willing to do. Once we know that it is possible in practice to decide whether or not something is a tautology (or an argument form is valid), the thing to do is to get *better* ways of doing it. And one way that is often (but not always) an improvement on truth tables is called the method of assigning values (MAV). The rationale is straightforward: to show that an argument form is valid (or that a formula is a tautology – we will consider this as a zero-premise argument for the moment), we must show that there is no evaluation in which the premises are true and the conclusion false. So, to show that, try to find such an evaluation. If there is one, it is not valid. If there isn't, it is valid. The method goes like this:

- Put a 0 under the main connective of the conclusion and a 1 under the main connective of the premises (if any).
- Then, work inward to the atomic propositions – put down the values of any other propositions that are forced by the ones you already have. If nothing is forced, write down two rows – one for each possibility.
- If you can complete this process, you have a counterexample to the validity of the argument. If not – that is, if you find you are forced to assign both 0 and 1 to some proposition – you know that it is valid.

Here is an example: we will test the argument from $((p \supset q) \mathrel{\&} (q \supset r)) \mathrel{\&} (r \supset s)$ to $(r \mathrel{\&} s) \supset p$. We write down the premise and the conclusion, with a line below, with a '1' under the main connective of the premise, and a '0' under the main connective of the conclusion:

((p ⊃ q) & (q ⊃ r)) & (r ⊃ s)	(r & s) ⊃ p
1	0

Then this forces more values. The conjunction in the premise is true, so both of its conjuncts are true. The conditional in the conclusion is false, so we must have the antecedent true and the consequent false:

((p ⊃ q) & (q ⊃ r)) & (r ⊃ s)	(r & s) ⊃ p
1 1 1	1 0 0

Then, other values are forced too. The p in the conclusion is false, so it must be false in the premise too. Similarly, the conjunction $((p \supset q)$ & $(q \supset r))$ is true, so both conjuncts must be true. Similarly, r & s must be true, so both r and s are true:

((p ⊃ q) & (q ⊃ r)) & (r ⊃ s)	(r & s) ⊃ p
0 1 1 1 1 1	1 1 1 0 0

The truth of r and s gives us values to distribute in the premises. These values are compatible with $r \supset s$ being true. (If we already knew that $r \supset s$ had to be false, we couldn't proceed, and then we'd know that the argument was valid, as we wouldn't be able to find a counterexample.) We can then let q be either true or false – it doesn't matter which. My choice is false, and we have the following completed table:

((p ⊃ q) & (q ⊃ r)) & (r ⊃ s)	(r & s) ⊃ p
0 1 0 1 0 1 1 1 1 1 1	1 1 1 0 0

So, the argument is not valid, as we have an evaluation satisfying the premise, but not the conclusion:

$$p = 0 \quad q = 0 \quad r = 1 \quad s = 1$$

Here is another case of MAV, this time testing the argument from $p \equiv q$ and $(q \,\&\, r) \equiv (p \vee r)$ to $q \equiv r$. We proceed as before, starting off by trying to set the premises as true and the conclusion false:

p	$\equiv$	q	$(q$	$\&$	$r)$	$\equiv$	$(p$	$\vee$	$r)$	q	$\equiv$	r
	1					1					0	

But now, we have some choices. No other value is forced by the values we have. For example, to make $q \equiv r$ false, we can either make q true and r false, or vice versa. So, we need two rows:

p	$\equiv$	q	$(q$	$\&$	$r)$	$\equiv$	$(p$	$\vee$	$r)$	q	$\equiv$	r
	1	1	1		0	1			0	1	0	0
	1	0	0		1	1			1	0	0	1

The values for q and r in each row then tell us the values of $q \,\&\, r$. The value of q gives us the value of p too, since $p \equiv q$ is set as true. So, our two cases look like this:

p	$\equiv$	q	$(q$	$\&$	$r)$	$\equiv$	$(p$	$\vee$	$r)$	q	$\equiv$	r
1	1	1	1	0	0	1	1		0	1	0	0
0	1	0	0	0	1	1	0		1	0	0	1

Now we are in trouble! Given the values of p and r, $p \vee r$ is true in each row. However, we want $(q \,\&\, r) \equiv (p \vee r)$ to be true, while having $q \,\&\, r$ false. We are stuck. There is no evaluation we can give $p \vee r$ to meet our demands. We mark this by writing 'x' in the spot:

p	$\equiv$	q	$(q$	$\&$	$r)$	$\equiv$	$(p$	$\vee$	$r)$	q	$\equiv$	r
1	1	1	1	0	0	1	1	1	× 0	1	0	0
0	1	0	0	0	1	1	0	×	1	0	0	1

This shows that there is no evaluation that makes $p \equiv q$ and $(q \& r) \equiv (p \vee r)$ both true while making $q \equiv r$ false. It follows that the argument is valid. We have

$$p \equiv q, (q \& r) \equiv (p \vee r) \vDash q \equiv r$$

This completes our tour of truth tables and the method of assigning values. You now have the basic tools required to check lots of different argument forms for validity. Try the exercises to practise your skills.

Summary

- To form a truth table for a formula, or an argument form, write down all the formulas in a row, with the atomic formulas occuring in these formulas to the left.
- Under the top row, add 2^n rows, where n is the number of atomic formulas. Then put all the different combinations of 0s and 1s under the atomic propositions to the left.
- Repeat these columns under the atomic propositions in each formula.
- Then work outwards using the truth tables for each connective. *You must remember these rules!*
- If you are testing one formula, the column containing the main connective of the formula is its value. If this column is all 1s, the formula is a *tautology*. If it is all 0s, the formula is a *contradiction*. Otherwise, it is *contingent*.
- If you are testing an argument form, the form is *valid* if and only if in every row in which the premises are true, so is the conclusion. It is *invalid* if and only if there is some row in which each premise is true and the conclusion is false.

- Each row of a truth table is an *evaluation* of the formulas. An argument form is valid if and only if there is no evaluation according to which the premises are true and the conclusion is false. Or equivalently, every evaluation satisfying the premises also satisfies the conclusion.
- We write '$X \vDash A$' to indicate that the argument form from X to A is valid.
- The *method of assigning values* is a technique for finding evaluations more quickly than listing all of them in a truth table. To test whether a formula is a tautology, you attempt to construct an evaluation that makes the formula false. If there is (at least) one, the formula is *not a tautology*. If there isn't one, the formula is a *tautology*.
- To test an argument form using the method of assigning values, try constructing an evaluation making the premises true and the conclusion false. If there is (at least) one, the argument form is *invalid*. If there isn't one, the argument form is *valid*.

Exercises

Basic

{3.1} Work out truth tables for the formulas in Exercise 2.6 in the previous chapter. You may not want to do all of them, but do them until you get the hang of them.

{3.2} Which of $p \supset ((p \supset q) \supset q)$, $p \vee (p \supset q)$, $(p \& (p \supset q)) \supset q$, $((p \& q) \supset r) \supset (p \supset r)$ and $((p \supset q) \supset p) \supset p)$ are tautologies?

{3.3} Two formulas are said to be *equivalent* iff they have the same truth value under any evaluations. In other words, if you do a combined truth table for both propositions, they have the same value in each row.

    1   Show that p and $\sim\sim p$ are equivalent.
    2   Show that $p \& q$ and $q \& p$ are equivalent.
    3   Show that $p \supset q$ and $\sim p \vee q$ are equivalent.
    4   Are any of $p \supset (q \supset r)$, $(p \supset q) \supset r$ and $\sim p \vee \sim(q \& \sim r)$ equivalent?
    5   Are any of $p \& \sim p$, $\sim(q \supset q)$, $r \vee \sim r$ and $s \supset s$ equivalent?

{3.4} Test these argument forms. Before testing them, note down your intuitive judgement of the validity of the argument. Then, compare your estimation with the result you get by truth tables (or MAV). Is there ever a conflict between your intuitive judgement and the result of truth tables? In these cases, can you explain the difference?

1. $p, p \supset q$ therefore q
2. p, q therefore $p \equiv q$
3. $p \& q$ therefore $p \equiv q$
4. $p, q \supset p$ therefore q
5. p, q therefore $p \& q$
6. p therefore $p \vee q$
7. $p \equiv q, p \equiv {\sim}q$ therefore ${\sim}p$
8. $p \supset (q \supset r)$ therefore $q \supset (p \supset r)$
9. $p \supset {\sim}p$ therefore ${\sim}p$
10. ${\sim}{\sim}p$ therefore p
11. $p \supset q$ therefore $(r \supset p) \supset (r \supset q)$
12. $p \supset q$ therefore ${\sim}q \supset {\sim}p$
13. p therefore ${\sim}p \supset q$
14. $p \supset (p \supset q)$ therefore $p \supset q$
15. p therefore $q \supset q$
16. $p \vee q, {\sim}q \vee r$ therefore $p \vee r$
17. $p \supset q$ therefore $q \supset p$
18. $p \supset (q \supset r)$ therefore $(p \supset q) \supset r$
19. $(p \& q) \supset r$ therefore $p \supset ({\sim}q \vee r)$
20. $p \supset q, r \supset s$ therefore $(q \supset r) \supset (p \supset s)$

{3.5} A radio commercial states: 'If you're thinking of orange juice but you're not thinking of *Orange Blossom*, then you're just not thinking of orange juice.' The advertisers seem to think that it follows that if you're thinking of orange juice, then you're thinking of *Orange Blossom*. Does this follow? (Hint: Let *j* stand for 'You're thinking of orange juice' and let *b* stand for 'You're thinking of *Orange Blossom*'. Test the resulting argument for validity.)

{3.6} 'We can't make life better for the starving without spending money on the problem. Therefore, if we spend money on the

51

problem, we can make life better for the starving.' Is this argument valid? Symbolise it and check its form.

{3.7} Immanuel Kant wrote: 'If a moral theory is studied empirically then examples of conduct will be considered. And if examples of conduct are considered, principles for selecting examples will be used. But if principles for selecting examples are used, then moral theory is not being studied empirically. Therefore, moral theory is not studied empirically.' Is this argument valid? Symbolise it and check its form.

{3.8} 'I will get a pet or buy a cuckoo clock. If I get a pet, I will get a monkey. I will buy a cuckoo clock only if I meet a persuasive clock salesman. Therefore, I won't both not get a monkey and not meet a persuasive clock salesman.' Is this argument valid? Symbolise it and check its form.

{3.9} 'If it rains this afternoon only if I don't need to water my plants then it rains this afternoon. Therefore, it rains this afternoon.' Is this argument valid? Symbolise it and check its form.

{3.10} 'If Josh works hard, he'll be able to buy a car, and if Emily studies hard, she'll be able to get a degree. Therefore, if Josh works hard, Emily will be able to get a degree, or if Emily studies hard, Josh will be able to buy a car.' Is this argument valid? Symbolise it and check its form.

{3.11} When we introduced disjunction, we noticed that sometimes it is used inclusively and sometimes it is used exclusively. We have seen the truth table for inclusive disjunction. Does exclusive disjunction have a truth table? If so, what is it?

Advanced

{3.12} Look back at your answers to Exercises 3.5–3.10. In any case, did you think that the translation into logical form made the argument valid when it was really invalid, or invalid when it was really valid? Can you think of any reasons that might explain this?

{3.13} A connective (write it as '•' for the moment) is *definable* in terms of other connectives if and only if there is some expression involving those other connectives that is equivalent to $p • q$.

1   Show that inclusive disjunction is definable in terms of conjunction and negation, by showing that $p \vee q$ is equivalent to $\sim(\sim p \ \& \sim q)$.

2   Define exclusive disjunction in terms of &, $\vee$ and $\sim$.

3   Define exclusive disjunction in terms of & and $\sim$.

4   Show that all of our connectives are definable in terms of & and $\sim$.

5   Show that all of our connectives are definable in terms of $\supset$ and $\sim$.

6   Show that not every connective is definable in terms of &, $\vee$ and $\supset$.

7   The 'Sheffer stroke' is defined with the table

p	q	$p \mid q$
0	0	1
0	1	1
1	0	1
1	1	0

(You can read $p \mid q$ as 'not both p and q'.) Show that every connective we have seen in this chapter is definable in terms of the Sheffer stroke.

8   List all possible truth tables of two-place connectives. There should be $2^4 = 16$, as there are two choices in each of the four slots of the table. Give names for each that somehow reflect their operations on truth values. Show that each connective in this list is definable by the Sheffer stroke, and by any of the sets $\{\&, \sim\}$, $\{\vee, \sim\}$ and $\{\supset, \sim\}$.

9   Show that not every connective is definable in terms of $\equiv$ and $\sim$.

{3.14} Work out truth tables for $(p \supset q) \vee (q \supset p)$, $(p \supset q) \vee (q \supset r)$, $(p \ \& \sim p) \supset q$, $p \supset (q \vee \sim q)$. Substitute arbitrary propositions for p, q and r (e.g. I'll become a world-famous logician, Queensland has won the Sheffield Shield . . .). What does this tell you about '⊃' as a translation of conditionals? Which of these formulas should come out as tautologies for the English conditional?

{3.15} Which of the following statements are correct? Explain and justify your answers in each case. In each statement, X and Y are sets of formulas, and A, B and C are each single formulas. So, you should read $X \vDash A$ as 'any evaluation satisfying everything in X also satisfies A' and $Y, A \vDash B$ as 'any evaluation satisfying everything in Y as well as A also satisfies B'.

1 If $X \vDash A$ and $Y, A \vDash B$ then $X, Y \vDash B$.
2 If $X \vDash A$ then $X \nvDash \sim A$.
3 If $X, A \vDash B$ and $X, \sim A \vDash B$ then $X \vDash B$.
4 If $X, A \vDash B$ then $X \vDash A \supset B$.
5 If $X \vDash A \supset B$ then $X, A \vDash B$.
6 If $X \nvDash A$ then $X \vDash \sim A$.
7 If $X, A \vDash C$ and $X, B \vDash C$ then $X, A \lor B \vDash C$.
8 If $X, A \mathbin{\&} B \vDash C$ then $X, A \vDash C$ or $X, B \vDash C$.
9 If $X, A \vDash C$ or $X, B \vDash C$ then $X, A \mathbin{\&} B \vDash C$.
10 If $X, A \vDash B$ and $X, A \vDash B$ then $X \vDash A \equiv B$.

> True and False are attributes of speech, not of things.
> And where speech is not,
> there is neither Truth nor Falsehood.
> – Thomas Hobbes

Chapter 4

Trees

Although the method of assigning values is a great improvement on truth tables, it too can get out of control. It often is difficult to keep track of what is going on, and you don't get too much of an idea of why the argument is valid or invalid – all you get is one counterexample, if there is one. We will introduce another method for evaluating arguments that is as quick and efficient as the method of assigning values, but is much easier to handle, and that gives you more information about the argument form you are considering. The structures we will use are called analytic tableaux, or, more simply, trees.

To introduce trees, it is helpful to get a good grip on the way validity of arguments works. The notation '⊨' for validity is important, and there is a little more that we can do with this idea of the consequence relation between premises and conclusions. Let's first summarise the definition:

> $X \vDash A$ if and only if any evaluation satisfying everything in X also satisfies A.

Or equivalently, if you prefer a negative statement, we have

> $X \vDash A$ if and only if there is *no* evaluation satisfying everything in X that doesn't satisfy A.

Now, this works for *any* collection X of formulas. In particular, it works when X is empty. We write this as '$\vDash A$'. What does this mean? Well, it means that any evaluation satisfying everything in the empty set also satisfies A. Well, satisfying everything in the empty set is really easy. (After all, there is nothing in the empty set for an evaluation to make false!) So '$\vDash A$' has this definition:

> $\vDash A$ if and only if any evaluation satisfies A.

So, $\vDash A$ if and only if A is a tautology. That is one use of '$\vDash$'. Another use is when we leave out the formula A. Here, $X \vDash$ holds if and only if there's no evaluation satisfying everything in X that doesn't satisfy ... *what*? There's nothing to satisfy in the conclusion. So we have this definition:

> $X \vDash$ if and only if there is no evaluation satisfying everything in X.

So, $X \vDash$ if and only if the set X is *unsatisfiable*. The guiding idea of trees is this result:

> $X \vDash$ if and only if there is no evaluation satisfying everything in X.

If the argument from X to A is valid then there is no evaluation making the premises X true and the conclusion A false. Therefore, there is no evaluation satisfying all of X and also $\sim A$, so $X, \sim A \models$. Conversely, if $X, \sim A \models$ then there is no evaluation making the premises X true and the conclusion A false, and so the argument is valid. We have $X \models A$.

The idea behind trees

The method for trees goes like this: to test an argument, put the premises of the argument and the *negation of the conclusion* in a list. We want to see if this list can be satisfied – if the propositions cannot be true together, the argument is valid; if they can be true together, the argument is not valid. So, trees test for satisfaction. To illustrate the technique of trees, we will test the argument from $p \supset q$ and $r \vee \sim q$ to $(p \vee q) \supset r$. We do this by writing down in a list the formulas we wish to be satisfied in order to show that the argument is invalid:

$$p \supset q$$
$$r \vee \sim q$$
$$\sim((p \vee q) \supset r)$$

Now we examine what must be done to make all these formulas true. The simplest consequence is this: to make $\sim((p \vee q) \supset r)$ true, $p \vee q$ must be true, and r must be false. In general, a conditional $A \supset B$ is false when A is true and B is false, so $\sim(A \supset B)$ is true, just when A and $\sim B$ are true. So, in our case, we can add $p \vee q$ and $\sim r$ to our list of things to satisfy. We do this by extending the list with a vertical line, adding the new propositions:

$$p \supset q$$
$$r \vee \sim q$$
$$\sim((p \vee q) \supset r) \checkmark$$
$$|$$
$$p \vee q$$
$$\sim r$$

We also tick $\sim\!((p \vee q) \supset r)$ to indicate that it has been processed, and that we have done everything required to ensure that it is true. Now, look at the disjunction $r \vee \sim\!q$. To make this true, we must make either r true or $\sim\!q$ true. This gives us two possibilities, and to indicate this, we branch the tree like this:

$$p \supset q$$
$$r \vee \sim\!q \checkmark$$
$$\sim\!((p \vee q) \supset r) \checkmark$$
$$|$$
$$p \vee q$$
$$\sim\!r$$

$$r \qquad \sim\!q$$
$$\times$$

We have ticked $r \vee \sim\!q$, as we have processed this formula and there is nothing else we can do with it. The tree now has two branches. The left branch goes from the top down to r, and the right branch goes from the top down to $\sim\!q$. If we can satisfy either of these lists of formulas, the argument is invalid. Now, one of the branches is unsatisfiable, since it contains a *contradiction*. The left branch contains both r and $\sim\!r$, and there is no way we will be able to satisfy both of these formulas. As a result, we say that this branch is closed, and we indicate that with a cross at the bottom.

Now we can continue the tree. We must deal with $p \supset q$ and $p \vee q$. To make $p \supset q$ true, we must make either p false (which means making $\sim\!p$ true) or q true. The tree branches again. We split the tree under every open branch. Here the only open branch is the left one:

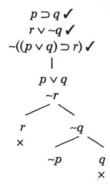

$$p \supset q \checkmark$$
$$r \vee \sim\!q \checkmark$$
$$\sim\!((p \vee q) \supset r) \checkmark$$
$$|$$
$$p \vee q$$
$$\sim\!r$$

$$r \qquad \sim\!q$$
$$\times$$
$$\sim\!p \qquad q$$
$$\times$$

Again, the right branch closes, this time because we have the contradictory pair q and $\sim q$. The left branch remains open. To complete the tree, we must process the disjunction $p \vee q$. This is simple. The tree splits again, with p in one branch and q in the other:

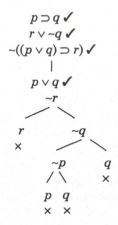

Both of the new branches close, as both p and $\sim p$ feature in the left branch, and q and $\sim q$ feature in the right branch.

As a result, there is no way to satisfy each of the formulas $p \supset q$, $r \vee \sim q$ and $\sim((p \vee q) \supset r)$. So, the argument from $p \supset q$ and $r \vee \sim q$ to $(p \vee q) \supset r$ is valid.

The completed tree for an argument gives you a picture of the reasoning used to show that the argument is valid (or to show that it is invalid). Trees are more 'clever' than truth tables, as they do not use the 'brute force' technique of listing all the different possibilities and checking the premises and conclusion in each possibility. Trees are more informative than MAV, because a completed tree gives you a record of the reasoning used. A completed tree is a *proof*.

Let's look at another example, before going on to define the tree rules precisely. To test to see whether a formula is a tautology, you check to see whether its negation is satisfiable. We want to show that this negated formula cannot be true. Here is an example, testing the formula $((p \supset q) \& q) \supset p$:

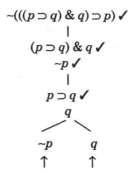

We start this tree with the negated formula, $\sim(((p \supset q)\ \&\ q) \supset p)$, at the top. To make this true, we make the antecedent $(p \supset q)\ \&\ q$ true and the consequent p false. So we added $(p \supset q)\ \&\ q$ and $\sim p$. Then, we process the conjunction: $(p \supset q)\ \&\ q$. Conjunctions are straightforward: you ensure that both conjuncts are true. So, we add $p \supset q$ and q to our tree. Finally, we process the conditional $p \supset q$, and for this we ensure either that $\sim p$ is true (the left branch) or that q is true (the right branch). Both branches of the tree stay open, and we indicate this with the vertical arrow at the bottom of the branches.

Both branches are said to be completed, and both are open. Therefore, both represent ways to satisfy the formula $\sim(((p \supset q)\ \&\ q) \supset p)$. Select a branch (I have chosen the left one), and read up that branch to find each atomic formula occurring by itself in the branch. These atomic formulas have to be true in the possibility in question. In the left branch, we have q. We do not have p occurring by itself. (If we did, it would close the branch with the $\sim p$.) So, in our evaluation, we make q true. Since $\sim p$ occurs in the branch, we make p false. These are the only atomic formulas in the branch, so the open branch on the left gives us the evaluation

$$p = 0 \quad q = 1$$

And indeed, this evaluation does not satisfy the formula $((p \supset q)\ \&\ q) \supset p$. Therefore, it is not a tautology.

Tree rules

The tree rules consist in the rules for resolving each kind of formula, and the rules for developing branches and closing them. First, we examine the resolving rules.

Double negation

To resolve a formula of the form ~~A, extend any open branch in which the formula occurs with the formula A. We write this in shorthand as

Conjunction

To resolve a formula of the form A & B, extend any open branch in which the formula occurs with the formulas A and B. We write this as

Negated conjunction

To resolve a formula of the form ~(A & B), extend any open branch in which the formula occurs with two new branches, one containing ~A and the other ~B. We write this as

~(A & B)
~A ~B

Disjunction

To resolve a formula of the form $A \lor B$, extend any open branch in which the formula occurs with two new branches, one containing A and the other, B. We write this as

Negated disjunction

To resolve a formula of the form $\sim(A \lor B)$, extend any open branch in which the formula occurs with the formulas $\sim A$ and $\sim B$. We write this as

Conditional

To resolve a formula of the form $A \supset B$, extend any open branch in which it occurs with two new branches, one containing $\sim A$ and the other containing B. We write this as

Negated conditional

To resolve a formula of the form $\sim(A \supset B)$, extend any open branch in which the formula occurs with the formulas A and $\sim B$. We write this as

Biconditional

To resolve a formula of the form $A \equiv B$, extend any open branch in which the formula occurs with two new branches, one containing A and B and the other $\sim A$ and $\sim B$. We write this as

$$
\begin{array}{ccc}
 & A \equiv B & \\
 \diagup & & \diagdown \\
 A & & \sim A \\
 B & & \sim B
\end{array}
$$

Negated biconditional

To resolve a formula of the form $\sim(A \equiv B)$, extend any open branch in which the formula occurs with two new branches, one containing A and $\sim B$ and the other $\sim A$ and B. We write this as

$$
\begin{array}{ccc}
 & \sim(A \equiv B) & \\
 \diagup & & \diagdown \\
 A & & \sim A \\
 \sim B & & B
\end{array}
$$

Each of these rules makes sense, given the truth table definitions of the connectives. If the formula to be resolved is true then one of the possibilities below it has to be true also. This will help you remember the rules.

Closure

A branch is closed when it contains a formula and its negation (the formula need not be atomic). A branch that is not closed is said to be open.

Partially developed trees

A partially developed tree for a set X of formulas is a tree starting with those formulas X (at the top), and in which some of the formulas have been resolved, in accordance with the resolving rules. Therefore, each formula in the tree is either in the set X or follows from formulas higher up in the tree by way of the resolving rules.

Completed trees

A completed tree for a set X of formulas is a partially developed tree in which, in every open branch, every formula has been resolved. (Note that we do not require that formulas in closed branches be resolved. If the branch is closed, we need not worry about resolving formulas that occur only in that branch, as that branch cannot be satisfied.)

New notation

We write '$X \vdash$' to indicate that a completed tree for X closes. We write '$X \nvdash$' to indicate that a completed tree for X remains open. We can write '$X \vdash A$' as shorthand for '$X, \sim A \vdash$' to indicate that a tree for the argument from X to A closes. (You might have noticed a problem with this definition: $X \vdash$ means 'a completed tree for X closes', $X \nvdash$ means 'a completed tree for X doesn't close'. What happens if some completed trees close, and others remain open? The rules give you flexibility in the order of applying the rules. Maybe some orders will give you a closed tree, and with others the tree remains open! Fortunately for us, and fortunately for the definition, this never happens. The order in which rules are applied makes no difference to whether the tree closes or not. In fact, in the section after next, we will show that if one completed tree for X closes, all do. And conversely, if one completed tree for X stays open, all do. So, our definition makes sense.)

Trees are a good technique for propositional logic if and only if $\vDash$ and $\vdash$ coincide. We will check that this is the case soon – but before

Box 4.1

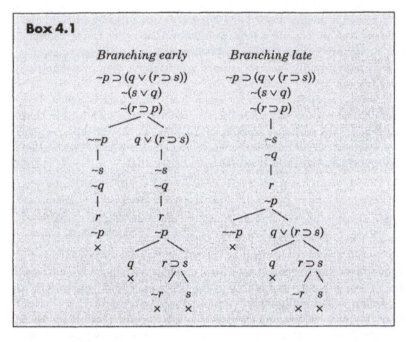

that, let's look at some more trees, to understand how to develop them efficiently and quickly.

Our first example is a pair of trees. Both show that $\sim p \supset (q \vee (r \supset s))$, $\sim(s \vee q) \vdash r \supset p$. The trees are presented in Box 4.1. In the tree on the left (*branching early*), we resolve the formulas in the order in which they appear. In the tree on the right (*branching late*), we apply the linear rules before the branching ones. You will see that both trees have the same *depth*. However, the tree with deferred branching has fewer formulas in total (17, compared with 13).

The moral of this example is clear: if you want your tree to close without growing too much, defer your branching as much as possible. Call rules that split the tree *branching rules*, and call the remaining rules *linear rules*. We then have the following moral:

Use the *linear* rules before the branching rules.

65

This moral is merely a word of advice. It is not a hard-and-fast rule, for only time and space is to be gained by keeping it. Using branching rules before linear rules will not result in a different answer – it will usually only lead to a more roundabout way of getting to that answer.

There is another lesson to learn from this pair of trees. If a branch closes, there is no need to resolve all of the formulas in that branch. In the leftmost branch of both trees, we did not resolve ~~p. Instead of resolving it, we used it to close with ~p. This closed the branch earlier than it would have otherwise.

> If you think the tree will close, apply rules that lead to closures.

This word of advice may sometimes conflict with the advice to use linear rules before branching rules. You may find yourself in a situation where applying a branching rule will result in a closure (perhaps of both branches), and this might well close the whole tree. In that case, it is clearly in your interest to apply this branching rule before any linear rules.

To illustrate these lessons further, we will test the argument from $(p \lor q) \equiv (r \& s)$ and $q \equiv (r \supset p)$ to $r \supset (p \lor q)$. The tree is shown in Box 4.2. This tree develops linearly until we process $(p \lor q) \equiv (r \& s)$. Then the left branch contains $p \lor q$ and $r \& s$. The first piece of advice would have us then process $r \& s$, but instead we follow the second piece of advice, to branch $p \supset q$, as both of these result in an immediate closure. The rest of the tree is processed in the same way. The rightmost branch remains open, and, as a result, we have an evaluation in which the premises are true and the conclusion false. Reading the values off the open branch indicated, we have

$$\text{Evaluation:} \quad p = 0 \quad q = 0 \quad r = 1 \quad s = 0$$

You can check for yourself that this evaluation indeed makes the premises true and the conclusion false. (It is a very good idea to do this whenever you complete a tree. If you made a mistake in the

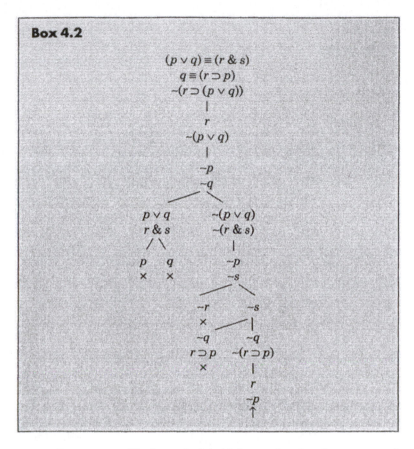

Box 4.2

$(p \lor q) \equiv (r \& s)$
$q \equiv (r \supset p)$
$\sim(r \supset (p \lor q))$
|
r
$\sim(p \lor q)$
|
$\sim p$
$\sim q$

$p \lor q$ $\sim(p \lor q)$
$r \& s$ $\sim(r \& s)$
/ \ |
p q $\sim p$
$\times$ $\times$ $\sim s$

$\sim r$ $\sim s$
$\times$

$\sim q$ $\sim q$
$r \supset p$ $\sim(r \supset p)$
$\times$ |
r
$\sim p$
↑

tree rules, you are likely to find it if the evaluation is wrong and
you checked it.)

Our final example is shown in Box 4.3. This tree shows how much
branching must sometimes be done, even when we follow our own
two words of advice. Here, the only linear rule to apply is the
negated conditional $\sim(r \supset (p \equiv q))$. Every other rule must branch,
and to close the tree, every other rule must be applied. The resulting tree is rather large. It has nine different branches, while a truth
table for this argument would only have eight rows! However, this
tree is not really more complex than the corresponding truth table.
A truth table for this argument would have eight rows, and $8 \times 15 =$
120 entries, and we must also calculate values for $8 \times 6 = 48$ entries

Box 4.3

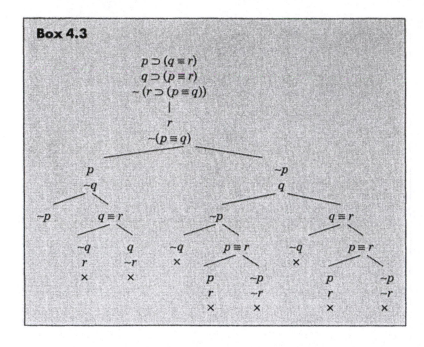

for the six connectives that appear. In contrast, this tree contains only 29 formulas, and we only performed only 8 resolving rules and 9 closures to complete the tree. The tree takes up more space on the page, but you are less likely to make a mistake in creating the tree than in the truth table. There are only 8 rules applied, as opposed to the 120 zeros and ones to be written in the truth table.

These examples should be enough to show you how to apply the tree rules correctly and to give you some idea of how to apply them efficiently. There are plenty of exercises at the end of this chapter for you to apply these skills. Before we get to the exercises, however, we must verify that the tree method gives the same results as truth tables.

Why the tree method works

We want to show that $\models$ and $\vdash$ come to the same thing. That is, we want to show first that if $X \vdash A$ (i.e. if the tree for $X, \sim A$ closes) then

$X \vDash A$ (i.e., any evaluation satisfying everything in X also satisfies A), and second that this goes in reverse: if $X \vDash A$ then $X \vdash A$. Since $X \vdash A$ comes to the same thing as $X, {\sim}A \vdash$, and since $X \vDash A$ comes to the same thing as $X, {\sim}A \vDash$, we can restrict ourselves to the case of *satisfiability* on the one hand and open trees on the other. That is, we will convince ourselves of two important facts:

Fact 1

If X is satisfiable then, in any totally developed tree for X, some branch remains open. That is, if $X \nvDash$ then $X \nvdash$.

Fact 2

If in some totally developed tree for X, some branch remains open then X is satisfiable. That is, if $X \nvdash$ then $X \nvDash$.

These two facts together have the nice consequence of proving that the order in which you apply the tree rules is irrelevant when it comes to closure of trees. By Fact 2, if some tree for X stays open then X is satisfiable. Then, by Fact 1, it follows that every tree for X remains open. Now we will prove both facts.

Proof of fact 1

If X is satisfiable, there is some evaluation that makes true every formula in X. We will call the evaluation I, and for any formula A made up of the atomic formulas that appear in X, we will write '$I(A)$' for the truth value that I assigns to A. Since X is satisfiable, if A is a sentence in X then $I(A) = 1$. If A is the negation of a sentence in X then $I(A) = 0$. Other sentences might be assigned 1 and others might be assigned 0. The important fact about evaluations is that for no sentence A at all do we have $I(A) = 1$ and $I({\sim}A) = 1$. If $I(A) = 1$ then I interprets ${\sim}A$ as false: $I({\sim}A) = 0$. Conversely, if I interprets ${\sim}A$ as true (so $I({\sim}A) = 1$) then we must have $I(A) = 0$.

We will show that in a completed tree for X, there is some branch in which every formula is satisfied by the evaluation I. It follows that this branch is open, since it can contain no contradictory pair of formulas A and $\sim A$, as these have to be satisfied by I. So, if we find such a branch, we are done: our tree contains an open branch.

Finding such a branch is quite simple. You start at the top of the tree, with the formulas in X. These are each satisfied by I, since that is what we assumed. Now, for each rule that is applied to extend the tree, at least one of the branches generated will give us formulas that are satisfied by I, provided that the formula resolved is also satisfied by I. We take the rules one at a time.

If we resolve a double negation $\sim\sim A$ then we know that $I(\sim\sim A) = 1$. The rule adds A to the branch, but we can see that $I(A) = 1$ too.

If we resolve a conjunction $A \& B$ then we know that $I(A \& B) = 1$. We add A and B to the branch, but clearly $I(A) = 1$ and $I(B) = 1$, so these formulas are satisfied too. If we resolve a negated conjunction $\sim(A \& B)$ then we have $I(\sim(A \& B)) = 1$, and so $I(A \& B) = 0$. We have two branches, one containing $\sim A$ and the other $\sim B$. Now, since $I(A \& B) = 0$, we must have either $I(A) = 0$ or $I(B) = 0$ (to make a conjunction false, you must make one of the conjuncts false). Therefore, we must have either $I(\sim A) = 1$ or $I(\sim B) = 1$. So, at least one of $\sim A$ and $\sim B$ is satisfied by I. Pick the branch that is satisfied by I and continue from there.

The other connective rules work in the same way. If we resolve a disjunction $A \vee B$ then we have $I(A \vee B) = 1$. We have two branches, one containing A and the other B. Now, since $I(A \vee B) = 1$, we must have either $I(A) = 1$ or $I(B) = 1$, so at least one of A and B is satisfied by I. Pick the branch that is satisfied by I and continue from there. If we resolve a negated disjunction $\sim(A \vee B)$ then we know that $I(A \vee B) = 0$. We add $\sim A$ and $\sim B$ to the branch, but since we must have $I(A) = 0$ and $I(B) = 0$, we have $I(\sim A) = 1$ and $I(\sim B) = 1$, so these formulas are satisfied too.

If we resolve a conditional $A \supset B$ then we have $I(A \supset B) = 1$. We have two branches, one containing $\sim A$ and the other B. Now, since $I(A \supset B) = 1$, we must have either $I(A) = 0$ or $I(B) = 1$, so at least one of $\sim A$ and B is satisfied by I. Pick the branch satisfied by I and continue from there. If we resolve a negated conditional $\sim(A \supset B)$ then we know that $I(A \supset B) = 0$. We add A and $\sim B$ to the branch, but since we must have $I(A) = 1$ and $I(\sim B) = 1$, these formulas are satisfied too.

Finally, for a biconditional $A \equiv B$, we have $I(A \equiv B) = 1$. We have two branches, one containing A and B and the other containing $\sim A$ and $\sim B$. Now, since $I(A \equiv B) = 1$, I must assign A and B the same truth value. If the value is 1, pick the left branch; if the value is 0, pick the right one. For a negated biconditional $\sim(A \equiv B)$, we have $I(A \equiv B) = 0$, and I assigns A and B different values. The tree has two branches, one containing A and $\sim B$, and the other $\sim A$ and B. One of these is satisfiable.

This completes the demonstration that, however the tree develops, we can always choose a branch satisfied by the evaluation I. Therefore, this branch will not close, and the tree remains open. We have established Fact 1.

We have actually established a little more than Fact 1. We have shown that any evaluation satisfying X will be found by any tree for X, in the sense that each evaluation satisfying X will have at least one branch such that each formula in that branch is satisfied by that evaluation. It follows that, in some sense, trees contain all the information contained in truth tables. They will find all the evaluations satisfying a formula – not just some of them. (However, some branches might be satisfied by more than one evaluation. Take the case of a tree for $p \vee q$. It has one branch including p, and another with q. There are three different evaluations of the atoms p and q that satisfy the disjunction, but only two open branches! This is because the p branch is satisfied by the evaluation ($p = 1$ and $q = 0$) *and* the evaluation ($p = 1$ and $q = 1$). This second evaluation satisfies the right branch too, along with ($p = 0$ and $q = 1$). The three evaluations are represented by two open branches.)

Now we must turn to Fact 2. If a tree for X remains open then we can construct an evaluation satisfying all of the formulas in X.

Proof of fact 2

It turns out that it is quite a bit easier to prove something slightly stronger than this fact. We will show that if you have an open branch in a totally developed tree for X then there is an evaluation satisfying *every formula in that branch*. This proves the result, since the formulas in X are sitting at the top of the tree, and they appear in every branch.

So, take your open branch. Call it O for the moment. Make an evaluation of propositions by assigning the following truth values to atomic formulas: $I(p) = 1$ if p is in the branch O, and $I(p) = 0$ if $\sim p$ is in the branch O. $I(p)$ can be whatever you like if neither p nor its negation appears in the branch O. (This definition does give us an evaluation, since the branch is not closed: we don't have p and $\sim p$ in the one branch. Therefore, we can assign our truth values consistently.)

We will show that this definition works, by showing for every formula A, if A is in O then $I(A) = 1$ and if $\sim A$ is in O then $I(A) = 0$.

The style of reasoning we will use is often called a *proof by induction*. This technique exploits the fact that every formula is built (by the connectives) out of atomic formulas. Given this fact, if you want to show that something holds of every formula, it is enough to show two things. First, that it holds of atomic formulas, and second, that if it holds of some formulas, it holds of the formulas you can make out of them too. If you can prove these two things, your property holds of every formula whatsoever. Let me illustrate with a simple example. We can conclusively prove that every formula has the same number of left parentheses as right parentheses. (This is obvious by glancing at the rules, but spelling out the proof is a good example of induction.) The item we want to prove is called the hypothesis. The hypothesis holds for atomic formulas, because each atomic formula has no left parentheses and no right parentheses. So, we have proved the first part, or what we might call the base case of the induction. For the second part, we show that if the hypothesis holds for a collection of formulas, it holds for each of the formulas we can make out of them, too. We can make formulas either by using negation or by using a two-place connective: &, $\vee$, $\supset$ or $\equiv$. In the case of negation, whatever the formula A is like, its negation $\sim A$ has the same number of left parentheses as A, and the same number of right parentheses as A too. So, if A has the same number of left and right parentheses, so does $\sim A$. In the case of combining two formulas together, such as $(A \mathbin{\&} B)$, if A has n left and n right parentheses, and B has m left and m right parentheses, then the conjunction $(A \mathbin{\&} B)$ has $1 + n + m$ left parentheses and $n + m + 1$ right parentheses. So the conjunction (or disjunction, conditional or biconditional) also has the same number of left and right parentheses. The result is proved. (It holds for the atoms. It holds for the formulas you can make up out of atoms using any one connective. It holds for the formulas you can make using these too. It holds for ones you can make out of this new bunch. And so on . . .)

Now let us continue with our proof: The hypothesis for this proof is this fact about the formula A in the open branch O: if A is in O then $I(A) = 1$, and if $\sim A$ is in O then $I(A) = 0$. We show that it holds for all formulas by first showing that it holds for atomic formulas. Then, to show that it holds in general, we suppose that it holds for some formulas, and we show that it holds for formulas you can make out of them. Then the hypothesis holds for any formula whatsoever. The hypothesis holds for the atomic formulas, since that is the way we defined I. If p is in O then $I(p) = 1$. If $\sim p$ is in O then $I(p) = 0$.

If the formula is a *conjunction* then if $A \,\&\, B$ is in O then, since we applied the conjunction rule to $A \,\&\, B$, A and B are in O. So $I(A) = 1$ and $I(B) = 1$, and as a result, $I(A \,\&\, B) = 1$ too. If $\sim(A \,\&\, B)$ is in O then either $\sim A$ is in O or $\sim B$ is in O. As a result, either $I(A) = 0$, or $I(B) = 0$, and in either case $I(A \,\&\, B) = 0$, as desired.

If the formula is a *disjunction* then if $A \lor B$ is in O then, since we applied the disjunction rule to $A \lor B$, either A or B is in O. So $I(A) = 1$ or $I(B) = 1$, and in either case, $I(A \lor B) = 1$ too. If $\sim(A \lor B)$ is in O then both $\sim A$ and $\sim B$ are in O, and as a result, both $I(A) = 0$, and $I(B) = 0$, giving $I(A \lor B) = 0$, as desired.

If the formula is a *conditional* then if $A \supset B$ is in O then, since we applied the implication rule to $A \supset B$, either $\sim A$ or B is in O. So $I(A) = 0$ or $I(B) = 1$, and in either case, $I(A \supset B) = 1$ too. If $\sim(A \supset B)$ is in O then both A and $\sim B$ are in O, and as a result, both $I(A) = 1$, and $I(B) = 0$, giving $I(A \supset B) = 0$, as desired.

For the *biconditional*, if $A \equiv B$ is in O then either A and B are in O or $\sim A$ and $\sim B$ are in O, and as a result, both $I(A) = I(B)$, giving $I(A \equiv B) = 1$, as desired. If $\sim(A \equiv B)$ is in O then either A and $\sim B$ are in O or $\sim A$ and B are in O, and as a result, $I(A)$ differs from $I(B)$, giving $I(A \equiv B) = 0$, as desired.

The only other formula left to consider is a double negation. If $\sim\sim A$ is in O then so is A. So, $I(A) = 1$, which gives $I(\sim A) = 0$, and $I(\sim\sim A) = 1$, which is what we want.

This deals with every kind of formula to be seen in our branch. Every formula in the branch is satisfied by I. As a result, the set X sitting atop the branch is satisfiable. This completes the proof of Fact 2.

These two facts jointly constitute what is *often* called a soundness and completeness proof for trees. Trees are a sound account for logic, as you cannot prove anything using trees which is not valid according to truth tables. Trees never go wrong (if $X \vdash$ then $X \models$). Trees are a complete account of logic, as you can prove anything using trees that is valid according to truth tables. Trees are always right.

Summary

- $X \models A$ if and only if $X,\sim A \models$. An argument from X to A is valid if and only if X together with $\sim A$ is unsatisfiable.
- Trees test for satisfiability. A tree for a set of formulas explores whether the set of formulas can be made true together.
- If a tree for X closes, we write '$X \vdash$'. If a tree for X remains open, we write '$X \nvdash$'.
- We write '$X \vdash A$' as shorthand for '$X,\sim A \vdash$'. A tree shows the argument from X to A to be valid if and only if the tree for $X,\sim A$ closes.
- Tree rules can be applied in any order, and you will get the same result each time. However, it is *often* good to delay the application of branching rules to get a smaller tree as a result.
- The tree method is sound. If $X \vdash A$ then $X \models A$. That is, if an argument is valid according to trees, it is valid according to truth tables too.
- The tree method is complete. If $X \models A$ then $X \vdash A$. That is, if an argument is valid according to truth tables, it is also valid according to trees.

Colin Howson's *Logic with Trees* [12] is an excellent introductory text featuring trees as its central motif. Another useful text is Bostock's *Intermediate Logic* [2]. Use Howson's book if you want more help getting used to trees, and use Bostock's if you want to explore trees more and to see how they compare with other techniques in formalising logic.

Smullyan's *First-Order Logic* [29] is a *tour de force* on the technique, and contains many insights into the use of trees. This book rewards detailed study.

Exercises

Basic

{4.1} Test all of the arguments from the exercises in Chapter 3 using trees. What are the advantages or disadvantages of using trees? In what cases do trees give you a quicker result? In what cases do trees take longer than truth tables or MAV?

{4.2} Find two tree rules appropriate for exclusive disjunction. (What do you do with an exclusive disjunction, and what do you do with a negated inclusive disjunction?)

{4.3} Find tree rules for the Sheffer stroke (see Exercise 3.13).

Advanced

{4.4} Prove soundness and completeness results for the tree rules for exclusive disjunction and the Sheffer stroke.

{4.5} Construct a new system of trees that uses the Sheffer stroke as the only connective in the language. This will require a radical reconstruction of the technique, as you no longer have negated connectives to treat differently to connectives. Every formula is either atomic or of the form $A \mid B$. What rules apply to formulas of the form $A \mid B$? How do branches close?

{4.6} Let's say that the size of a tree is the number of formulas occurring in the tree. Let's say that the size of a truth table is the number of truth values that get written down. Show that there is a formula such that any tree showing that it is a tautology has a greater size than that of a truth table showing that it is a tautology.

{4.7} Write a computer program that generates a tree for an argument specified by the user. Try to make it efficient, so that it produces a short tree when one is there to be found.

> Indeed, history is nothing more than a
> tableau of crimes and misfortunes.
> – Voltaire

Chapter 5

Vagueness and bivalence

The theory of logical consequence constructed so far is powerful and useful. It is elegant in its simplicity, but far-reaching in its power and its breadth. There are also some important problems for interpreting and using this account. In this chapter, we will look at one class of problems, which stem from the assumption that each proposition is assigned either the value 'true' or the value 'false'. This is the doctrine of bivalence ('bivalent' means 'has two values'). The first problem stems from the vagueness inherent in our use of language.

The problem of vagueness

Consider a long strip, shading continuously from scarlet at the left end to lemon yellow at the right end. It is divided into 10,000 regions – enough that any two adjacent regions look identical to you. Let r_1 be the proposition 'region 1 looks red to you', where region 1 is the leftmost patch, r_2 is 'region 2 looks red to you', and

77

so on, up to $r_{10,000}$. Because any two adjacent patches are indiscernibly different in colour, $r_1 \supset r_2$ is true. So is $r_2 \supset r_3$, and $r_{500} \supset r_{501}$, and so on, up to $r_{9,999} \supset r_{10,000}$. Region 5,000 probably does not look red to you. It will be some kind of orange if the strip shades evenly from red to yellow. Nonetheless, region 5,000 and region 5,001 do not differ in appearance to your eye, so you can agree that if region 5,000 is red, so is region 5,001. Therefore $r_{5,000} \supset r_{5,001}$ is true. The other conditionals $r_i \supset r_{i+1}$ are just as true. Now, because the leftmost edge is scarlet, r_1 is true. Therefore each of the premises in the following argument is true:

$$r_1, r_1 \supset r_2, r_2 \supset r_3, \ldots, r_{9,999} \supset r_{10,000}, \text{ therefore, } r_{10,000}$$

But this argument is *valid*, as you can check. It follows that the lemon-yellow end of the strip also looks red to you.

Enough of strips of colour. Consider a heap of grains of sand. Take away one solitary grain from the heap – you still have a heap, for one grain of sand is not enough to make the transition from heap to non-heap. So, if a pile of 10,000 grains of sand makes a heap (call this statement $h_{10,000}$) then a pile of 9,999 grains also makes a heap. So, $h_{10,000} \supset h_{9,999}$ is true. Similarly, $h_{9,999} \supset h_{9,998}$ is true, and so on. Given that 10,000 grains *does* make a heap, it follows via the argument

$$h_{10,000}, h_{10,000} \supset h_{9,999}, h_{9,999} \supset h_{9,998}, \ldots, h_2 \supset h_1, \text{ therefore, } h_1$$

that one solitary grain of sand makes a heap.

Similar lines of reasoning can be given to prove that no matter how little hair one has, one isn't bald (after all, removing one hair doesn't make you bald), that chickens have always existed (whatever is the parent of a chicken must also be a chicken), and that you are always a child (there is no day of transition between childhood and non-childhood). These are all called sorites arguments.[1] The problem they pose is called the *sorites paradox* because we seem to have a valid argument from obviously true premises to an obviously false conclusion.

How should we handle sorites arguments? They are genuine problems for the following reasons:

- The premises seem true.
- The argument seems valid.
- The conclusion seems false.

At this point, you might smell a rat. After all, we are using logic on what are vague notions. There seems to be no sharp borderline between red and yellow, heap and non-heap, bald and hairy, chicken and non-chicken, and child and adult, yet the technique of truth tables assumes that there is a sharp borderline. Any evaluation of propositions assumes that each proposition is assigned the value true or the value false. This seems to be in tension with the idea of applying logic to vague concepts.

Alternatives

What response are we to make of this? There seem to be a number of different responses to make (I owe this typology to John Slaney [27]):

1   Deny that the problem is legitimately set up. That is, hold that logic does not apply to vague expressions.
2   Accept that logic does legitimately apply here but hold that this particular argument is invalid.
3   Accept both that logic applies in such cases and that the argument is valid, but deny one of the premises.
4   Accept the argument and the premises, and hence embrace the conclusion also.

This seems to exhaust the options. Any response to the sorites paradoxes must respond along one of these four general lines. Each of these responses has its own difficulties, and this is why the sorites paradoxes are so difficult and yet so important to our understanding of logic. In the rest of this section, we will examine each line of response.

Option 1 has a heritage in philosophical circles, at the turn of the twentieth century in the work of philosophical logicians such as Frege and Russell. However, it is increasingly difficult to maintain, for the number of non-vague expressions seems rather small, and is perhaps limited to (parts of) mathematics. If Option 1 is to be taken, logic has an exceedingly limited application.

It may be tempting to say that logic has only to do with the precise, but the consequence seems to be that reasoning has no place in discourse about the vague. That is an extremely radical position. If I cannot reason about colour, shapes and sizes, baldness and heaps, species terms, and any other vague concept, I cannot do a lot of reasoning at all. Surely there is some standard by which to measure our reasoning, even when it uses vague concepts. Something must tell us that the sorites argument is unsound. If not, then we must reject the use of vague terms altogether.

Option 4 seems similar in thrust. If I hold that what looks yellow also looks red, that single grains of sand make heaps, that hirsute people are bald, then I am rejecting the standard use of vague concepts. This position is clearly very hard to maintain. It would seem to follow that nearly everything is true.

Options 2 and *3* are more mainstream, and seem to be the predominant views on vagueness.

Option 2 is plausible. The sorites arguments do seem quite fishy, and it is tempting to say that they are invalid. There are cases where the premises are true and the conclusion false. To model this, you must reject the traditional two-valued truth-table definition of logical consequence. Richer models must be used to give evaluations that make the premises true and the conclusion false.

One approach that attempts to do this is commonly called *fuzzy logic*. According to this account, truth values aren't simply 0 or 1 – they can be any number *between* 0 and 1. Propositions can be more or less true. Truth values come in 'shades of grey', with propositions being rather true (say, around 0.7), middling (around 0.5), not true at all (around 0.2), as well as genuinely true (1) and genuinely false (0), and all shades in between.

The logical connectives are still operations on truth values, but they are more complex now that you have more values to use. A negation $\sim A$ has (on the standard view) a value of 1 minus the value of A. A conjunction $A \mathbin{\&} B$ has the smaller of the two values of A and B. A standard account of implications is that $A \supset B$ is false only to the extent of how much falser B is than A. So, if B

is truer than A then $A \supset B$ has value 1. If A is 0.5 and B is 0.3 then $A \supset B$ is $0.8 = 1 - 0.2$, as you suffer a drop of 0.2 in going from the antecedent to the consequent.

The argument forms involved in sorites paradoxes are simply extended versions of modus ponens (from p, $p \supset q$ to derive q), and this argument form is about as well attested as any argument form can get. To take this line, you must be very careful to ensure that you do not throw out the logical baby with the sorites bathwater.

A fuzzy logic approach to the sorites argument can go like this. The proposition r_1 is just true (has value 1) and $r_{10,000}$ is just false (has value 0). Each conditional $r_i \supset r_{i+1}$ has a value that is very *very* close to 1, since the values of the proposition r_i decrease as i goes from 1 up to 10,000, and the value of a conditional is the drop in truth value from the antecedent to the consequent. So the premises are all either completely true or *very* close to it. The conclusion, on the other hand, is completely false. The argument is then invalid, as the truth (near enough) of the premises does not make the conclusion anywhere near true.

This view has its proponents. However, it also has its own difficulties. One is that vague propositions, on this approach, don't seem to be *really* vague. Take our series of 10,000 colour patches. It will still be true that there's some patch i such that r_i takes a value of 1 (it's really true) and r_{i+1} takes a value of slightly less than 1 (it's just a tad less than really true). So, there is a last *really truly* red patch. This is a strange conclusion to have. We seem to reject first-order borderlines, only to reinstate them at the next level. There is no sharp borderline between red and non-red, but there is a sharp borderline between really red and not really red.

Another odd consequence is the fact that since every sentence gets a value between 0 and 1, for every pair of vague propositions, one is truer than the other, or they have the same degree of truth. That may be fine for the same property (any two things are either exactly as red as each other or one is redder than the other), but for comparing different properties, it sounds silly. What does it mean to say that I'm tall to exactly the same degree as something is red? And while I am complaining, I may as well ask this: What does it mean to say that I am tall to degree 0.234205466453 . . .? What could numbers so precise mean anyway?

There are other ways to develop Option 2, but that has been enough to give you a flavour of the style of response that is possible. Let's move on to the only remaining response.

Option 3 is perhaps the orthodoxy in philosophical circles. It has all the advantages of not having to modify your logical theories, but it has the disadvantage of requiring us to pinpoint a false premise in an exceedingly plausible-looking bunch. In current research, there seem to be two main ways to develop this option. One way to do this is called the method of *supervaluations* (due originally to Bas van Fraassen [7]). According to this account, our concept 'red' does not pin down the location of the borderline between red and yellow. There is a range of *acceptable* borderlines, each as good as the other. We run our argument through many times, at each time, sharpening the borderline at a different place. If it is valid on all of these sharpenings, it works, and if it is invalid at some sharpening, it fails. Furthermore, if a statement is true on all sharpenings, it is true; if it is false on all sharpenings, it is false; and if it is true on some and false on some others, it suffers from a 'truth-value gap'. This is because our original concept 'red' is vague. It is not able to decide on whether or not this statement was true.

Undoubtedly, this proposal has some 'ring of truth' about it. According to the proposal, one of the premises are false (for, on every sharpening, one premise is false), but which one is never determinate. If this satisfies you as a solution then you are in good company. It might fail where it makes statements such as 'there is a patch such that it is red, and the next one is not' or 'there is a day such that on that day you are a child, but on the next, you are not' true. These statements seem to be false, and they also seem to be against the spirit of the supervaluational account – after all, it is motivated by the idea that more than one borderline is possible. So, it seems worthwhile to search for an alternative scheme for analysing the problem of vagueness.

One such alternative is called *epistemicism*. It has been championed by Timothy Williamson, in his excellent book, *Vagueness* [31]. Williamson bites the bullet, and holds that there *is* a real borderline between red and non-red, there is a single last day on which you are young, and a single first day on which you are old (these might not be the same day, of course). So much is a logical consequence of the fact that you are young when you are born, and you are not young when you are 80 years of age. Instead of attempting to do away with the borderlines as given by supervaluations, *epistemicism* states that they are there, but that the distinctive mark of vagueness is that these borderlines are *unknowable*. Something is 'epistemic' if it has to do with knowledge; hence, epistemicism is appropriately so-called, because, for epistemicism, borderline cases of red are those that we cannot know to be red or know to be non-red.

How is this plausible? One can reason like this: nothing except for our own practices in using the language is there to pin down the concepts 'red', 'young', 'bald' and others like them. Our faculties for discrimination pick out these concepts. This means that certain canonical cases are known to be red, and others are known to be not red. Our practices of discrimination ensure that there *is* a borderline, but our own capacities do not allow us to discern that borderline, because we are not able to determine such fine distinctions. Furthermore, the kinds of practices involving discriminating colours ensure that if we can tell that x is red, and if x is sufficiently similar in colour to y then y is red too. It follows that we cannot know what all the red things are, for this *has* a borderline, and we would not be able to discriminate between things close to the borderline.

What does the epistemicist say about the sorites argument? For the epistemicist, not all premises of the sorites argument are true. There *is* a last red patch. There *is* a pile of grains that makes a heap, but that is not a heap when one is removed. However, we have no way (and perhaps *can* have no way) to determine which colour patch or which number of grains is the borderline.

You may not agree with epistemicism (or with any of the other positions on the way to treat vagueness), but when evaluating positions you must remember that for *each* of the different accounts of how logic works, the values taken by propositions (such as 1 or 0, or the more extensive range of values in fuzzy logic) represent *truth* and *falsity* (and perhaps things in between), and not our own states of *knowledge*. We all agree that we are ignorant of some truths, and this means that some things might be true even though we do not know them to be true. If this is the case then, at least *some* times, propositions have a value 1 without that value representing the fact that it is known. The standard two-valued picture does not rule out ignorance or undecidability in analysing every proposition as being true or false. Ignorance and undecidability can remain when we say that it could be that something is true without our knowledge of that fact.

There is much more that can be said (and has been said) on this topic. The case is by no means closed. Consult some of the texts mentioned at the end of this chapter to explore the issues further.

Other problems with bivalence

Of course, vagueness is not the only problem to press against the doctrine of bivalence. There are many more. Here are just a few:

Paradox

Propositions such as 'this sentence is not true' (this is the *liar paradox*) and 'the set of non-self-membered sets is self-membered' (this is *Russell's paradox*) raise problems for the principle of bivalence. It seems impossible to consistently assign these propositions truth values. If 'this sentence is not true' is true then what it says is wrong, so it is not true. This is just what it says, so it is true. So, if it is true, it is not true; and if it is not true, it is true. What are we to say about this? Is it a proposition? Is it true? Is it not true? There is no simple answer to this.

Non-denoting terms

What should we say about claims that purport to refer to objects when there really is no object to which to refer. An example is 'The present king of France is bald'. France has no king at present, so the term 'the present king of France' does not denote. It is a non-denoting term. Is the proposition including the term true? Surely not. There is no present king of France to be bald, so it cannot be true. But is it false? If I say that the present king of France is not bald then I am just as surely talking about the present king of France. Neither response seems appropriate. (We will discuss this difficulty in Chapter 12, when we get some more logical material under our belt to use to analyse what might be going on.)

Presupposition failure

Non-denoting terms are an example of a more general problem of presupposition failure. We seem to have a presupposition that our terms pick out objects. When that presupposition fails, we have problems interpreting claims involving those terms. Other sorts of presupposition failure also seem to generate tension with the principle of bivalence. For example, if I presuppose that you have been involved in domestic violence, and I ask you 'have you stopped beating your spouse', then no 'yes/no' response seems appropriate if you have never beaten your spouse. (Let alone if you do not have a spouse.) In these cases, 'I have stopped beating my spouse' seems neither true (as you have not even started) or false (for you are not continuing to beat him or her).

Future contingents

A final example dates back to Aristotle, who noted that we are loath to assign truth values to what we might call future contingents [18]. These are statements about the future, such as 'There will be a sea battle tomorrow', which may become true, and may become false. There is a long-standing tradition to treat these as neither true nor false now but somehow awaiting the assignment of their truth value.

Further reading

Chapter 7 in Read's *Thinking About Logic* [21] is a helpful short survey of the issues surrounding vagueness. Williamson's book *Vagueness* [31] is not only a spirited defence of epistemicism, but also a fair-minded generous overview of competing positions. Jan Łukasiewicz (a Polish logician who worked in the first half of the twentieth century) is responsible for what are probably the most popular truth tables involving more than two values. His essay 'On determinism' [18] in his collected works is a readable account motivating *three*-valued tables for future contingents. The tables for conjunction, disjunction, implication and negation are as follows:

p	q	$p \& q$	$p \vee q$	$p \supset q$	$\sim p$
0	0	0	0	1	1
0	1/2	0	1/2	1	1
0	1	0	1	1	1
1/2	0	0	1/2	1/2	1/2
1/2	1/2	1/2	1/2	1	1/2
1/2	1	1/2	1	1	1/2
1	0	0	1	0	0
1	1/2	1/2	1	1/2	0
1	1	1	1	1	0

His *infinitely* valued logic has been popularised as *fuzzy logic*.

Slaney's 'Vagueness revisited' [27] is hard to find, but is perhaps the most sophisticated non-classical approach to vagueness. It attempts to circumvent the obvious difficulties with fuzzy logic. (If you cannot get 'Vagueness revisited', a little of the approach can be found in his 'A general logic' [28].)

For further criticism of fuzzy logic, consult Susan Haack's *Deviant Logic, Fuzzy Logic* [10].

Exercises

Basic

{5.1} A formula is said to be an Ł₃ tautology if and only if it has a value 1 under every evaluation in the three-valued truth tables given above. Each of the following formulas is a two-valued tautology. Which are Ł₃ tautologies?

$$p \vee \sim p \quad \sim(p \& \sim p) \quad p \supset ((p \supset q) \supset q) \quad (p \& (p \supset q)) \supset q$$
$$(p \supset r) \supset ((p \& q) \supset r)) \quad (p \supset \sim p) \supset \sim p \quad (p \supset q) \supset (\sim q \supset \sim p)$$
$$(p \& \sim p) \supset q \quad p \supset (\sim p \supset q) \quad ((p \supset q) \supset p) \supset p$$

Advanced

{5.2} Explain how you can use Lukasiewicz's three-valued logic to model statements about the future. What seems to 'fit badly' in such a modelling?

{5.3} Explain how you could use supervaluations to model statements about the future. What seems to 'fit badly' in such a modelling?

> Everything that can be thought at all
> can be thought clearly.
> – Ludwig Wittgenstein

Note

1 'Sorites' comes from the Greek word *soros*, meaning 'heap'. 'Sorites' is pronounced sor-eye-tees.

Chapter 6

Conditionality

Whenever you first see truth tables, one connective is more troublesome than any of the others: implication. The conditional $p \supset q$ is false only when p is true and q is false. This does not seem to fit with the way that we use 'if'. What can be said about this?

The paradoxes of material implication

The validity of argument forms like these

$$p \vDash q \supset p \quad p \vDash {\sim}p \supset q$$

follows immediately from the truth table rules for $\supset$. The problem with these argument forms is that they seem to have many *invalid* instances. Consider the argument from p to $q \supset p$. One instance is the inference from *I am alive* to *if I am dead, I am alive*. The premise is true, but the conclusion seems manifestly false. People are *not* alive when they are dead. Other instances lead you from *it's*

Tuesday to *if it's Wednesday it's Tuesday*, from *John Howard is Prime Minister of Australia* to *if John Howard is loses the election, John Howard is Prime Minister of Australia*.

The second form, from *p* to *~p ⊃ q*, fares no better. Instances lead you from *I'm alive* to *if I'm not alive, I'm famous*, or to *if I'm not alive, everyone is happy*, and, equally well, to *if I'm not alive, everyone is sad*. Each of these instances seems to lead one from truth to falsehood.

These argument forms are so troubling that they have been given a name – the *paradoxes of material implication*. There are more paradoxes than these two. The next argument form is also valid:

$$(p \, \& \, q) \supset r \vDash (p \supset r) \vee (q \supset r)$$

However, this argument also seems to have many invalid instances. Consider a case in which two switches must be thrown to turn on a light. The premise is

If switch 1 is on, and switch 2 is on, then the light is on.

The argument form indicates that we can infer

Either if switch 1 is on, the light is on, or if switch 2 is on, the light is on.

But this seems false. Both switches must be on for the light to be on – neither is sufficient in itself.

Another bizarre example is the tautology

$$\vDash (p \supset q) \vee (q \supset r)$$

Pick three propositions at random. By this tautology, it follows that either if the first of your propositions is true, so is the second, or if the second is true, so is your third – no matter how unrelated these propositions might be. For example: *Either, if the Pope is a Catholic, Queensland wins the Sheffield Shield, or if Queensland wins the Sheffield Shield, the moon is made of green cheese*. Is that true?

Given the paradoxes of material implication, there are two broad responses that could be made.

- The truth table for '⊃' is a good model for the truth values of conditionals. We then should attempt to explain why the paradoxes seem odd.
- The truth table for '⊃' is not a good model for the truth values of conditionals. The gap between '⊃' and 'if' then explains why the paradoxes seem so odd.

This chapter will examine both kinds of response to the paradoxes of material implication.

Truth and assertibility

The most popular response that maintains that '⊃' really does give us the truth table of the conditional does this by exploiting the distinction between truth and assertibility. A proposition is true if what it says is the way things are. A proposition is assertible if it is appropriate or reasonable to assert. These two notions come apart drastically. H. P. Grice, in his 'Logic and conversation' [9] gave an account of the rules governing assertibility in conversation. Most of his rules are common sense. You ought to make assertions you believe to be true, and not make assertions you believe to be untrue. Of course, what I believe to be true might not in fact be true (I am not infallible). Therefore, some things might be assertible but not true. Similarly, there are many things that are true but that I do not believe (I do not have an opinion on everything). Therefore, some things are true that are not assertible.

For our purposes, the difference between truth and assertibility is most important when we consider Grice's maxim of relevance. I ought not say more than is necessary, and I ought not say less than is necessary. If someone asks me how far it is to Canberra, and the context makes clear that they are planning to drive there, then if I quote the distance down to the last millimetre, I am being needlessly overinformative. I am saying more than is required. On the other hand, if I indicate that the distance is somewhere between 50 and 5,000 kilometres, when I know very well that it is around 300 kilometres, then I am being much less informative than required. In neither case is what I am saying untrue. However, in both cases what I say is not assertible.

Then, the response continues: The inference from p to $q \supset p$ seems odd because we hardly ever assert $q \supset p$ on the grounds that p. If I am asked

Did Queensland win the Sheffield Shield?

and I respond

If I'm going out to dinner tonight they did.

purely on the grounds that they *did* win, the questioner will think I'm being stupid. I have broken the maxim of relevance. Of course, if I knew that they did win, according to the classical account of 'if', my statement is actually *true*. It is just not *appropriate*. The only conditions in which it is appropriate to assert $p \supset q$ is when I am neither sure that p is false nor sure that q is true. For, in these cases, I ought to assert $\sim p$ or I ought to assert q. It is needlessly uninformative to merely assert $p \supset q$.

This account attempts to explain our hesitancy at the inference from p to $q \supset p$, and that from p to $\sim p \supset q$. (At least, it explains it in cases when we know or believe the premise of the argument. It is less clear that it explains our hesitancy to infer $q \supset p$ in cases where we merely *suppose p* to be true.) However, it seems clear that this argument cannot stay as it is here. In the same conversational situation as in the previous example, the questioner would think I was equally crazy to say

Either I'm going out to dinner tonight or they did.

but we have nothing like the same quarrel with the inference q therefore $p \vee q$. Our hesitancy at inferring $p \supset q$ from q is much stronger than our hesitancy at inferring $p \vee q$ from q (at least, once we make it clear that disjunction is read inclusively and not exclusively).

One development of the Gricean response is given by Frank Jackson, who argues that the assertibility of a conditional $p \supset q$

varies with the conditional probability $Pr(q|p)$ (this is the probability that q obtains, given that p obtains).[1] Jackson argues that, given the special role that conditionals play in our own reasoning (such as in dealing with hypothetical situations, and their use in the context of limited information), conditionals ought to be robust in the context of increasing information, and that this motivates the definition of its assertibility in terms of conditional probability. The details of Jackson's argument do not concern us here.

This response tells us something significant about the difference between conditionals and disjunction. As the probability of q goes up, so does that of $p \lor q$. However, as the probability of q goes up, it does not always follow that the probability $Pr(q|p)$ rises. (If it is more likely that Queensland wins the Sheffield Shield, it does not follow that it is more likely that they win the Sheffield Shield given that the team is stricken with influenza.)

However, even though Jackson's account of assertibility of conditionals does clarify things considerably, it does not at all deal with the assertibility of propositions in which conditionals are embedded. The proposition $(p \supset q) \lor (q \supset r)$ is a tautology, and hence has a probability 1. It does not seem assertible. Something must be said about the assertibility of disjunctions of conditionals, and other embeddings of conditionals. This theory does well for 'bare' conditionals, but this is only a very small part of the complex way conditionals function in language.

Possibilities

In Section 3.1, we argued that the conditional 'if p then q' had the same truth table as the negated conjunction $\sim(p \& \sim q)$. Let me repeat the argument here, but I shall now write 'if p then q' as '$p \rightarrow q$', to make clear that we are not necessarily assuming the material conditional, but arguing that the conditional we use *is* the material conditional. Here is the argument:

- If $p \rightarrow q$ is true then if p is true, q must be true (that is what a conditional says, after all) so you do not have p true and q false, so $p \& \sim q$ is not true, and consequently $\sim(p \& \sim q)$ is true.

- Conversely, if ~(p & ~q) is true, consider what happens if p is true. In that case, you don't have q false, since p & ~q is not true (that is what we have assumed: ~(p & ~q) is true.) So, if you don't have q false, q must be true. So, if p is true, so is q. In other words, p → q is true.

This is quite a powerful argument. If we wish to *reject* the identification of → with ⊃, we must block this argument somewhere. Most people agree with the first part of the argument. If the antecedent of a conditional is true and the consequent is false then the whole conditional is false. Conversely, if the conditional p → q is true then it is not the case that p and ~q. So, we ought to have

$$p \rightarrow q \vDash \sim(p \ \& \ \sim q)$$

The problems arise with the *second* part of the argument, where we attempt to move from ~(p & ~q) to p → q. Let's run through that argument, with an example in mind. Let p be *I'm dead* and let q be *I'm alive*. Then ~(p & ~q) is certainly true (I'm not both dead and not alive) but p → q seems false (it's not true that *if I'm dead, I'm alive*). With this example in mind, we will hopefully see where the argument breaks down.

The reasoning starts:

- If ~(p & ~q) is true, consider what happens if p is true. Well, what happens when p is true is that I'm dead. So, that is the case I must consider. The reasoning continues.
- In that case, you don't have q false, since p & ~q is not true (that is what we have assumed . . .). This seems *wrong*. In the situations in which I *am* dead, we *do* have q false. The reasoning presumes that we can still call on the truth of our original assumption ~(p & ~q) in a situation in which we have assumed that p is true. That is not appropriate in the example we are considering. If I am *dead*, it is no longer true that *I'm not both dead and not alive*.

So, to derive q in this case, we must have more than simply ~(p & ~q). For we wish to use ~(p & ~q) not only in our original situation, but *also* in the alternative situation we have hypothesised. The assumption we have made must be *robust,* in the sense that it survives into the new context in the discourse. One analysis of the conditional that attempts to make use of this observation says that the conditional $p \to q$ should be defined as

$$\Box \sim (p \ \& \ \sim q)$$

where '$\Box$' is a new one-place connective of *necessity.* $\Box \sim (p \ \& \ \sim q)\Box$ says that it is not merely an accident that $\sim (p \ \& \ \sim q)$. We have $\sim (p \ \& \ \sim q)$ not only in our situation, but in other possible situations too.

The connective $\Box$ is not truth-functional. That is, the truth of $\Box A$ does not depend merely on the truth value of A. The connective is said to be a *modal* operator, as it gives us a different mode for a proposition to be true, or asserted. Some propositions p might be true, while $\Box p$ is false (p might be true by *accident*). Other propositions p might be true with $\Box p$ true. The value of $\Box p$ depends on more than just the value of p. If we want to use a connective like $\Box$, we must expand the way formulas are interpreted.

One way to do this is to read $\Box p$ as 'no matter how things are, p is true', and to take the talk of ways things are rather literally. A modal evaluation is not just an assignment of truth values to propositions. It is an assignment of truth values to propositions in different *states*. We will follow the general convention and call these states *worlds*. Every evaluation comes with a set W of worlds at which propositions are true or false. We write

$$w \Vdash A \qquad w \nVdash A$$

to indicate that A is true in world w and that A is not true in world w respectively. Note that we now have three similar symbols: $\vDash$, $\vdash$ and now $\Vdash$. The first two relate sets of formulas to formulas: '$X \vDash A$' says that any evaluation satisfying X satisfies A too, and '$X \vdash A$' says that the tree for $X, \sim A$ closes -- that is, we have a proof that A follows from X. This new symbol is read like this: '$w \Vdash A$' means that the formula A is true at the world w.

Given some collection W of worlds, we define our evaluation by first setting the truth values of the atomic propositions in each world. This is done completely arbitrarily. Then, we use the same rules as before for each connective. For conjunction, disjunction and negation, we have the following evaluation conditions:

- $w \Vdash A \& B$ if and only if $w \Vdash A$ and $w \Vdash B$.
- $w \Vdash A \lor B$ if and only if $w \Vdash A$ or $w \Vdash B$.
- $w \Vdash {\sim}A$ if and only if $w \nVdash A$.

This is just a fancy new way of rewriting what we have already seen in truth tables. A conjunction is true (at world w) if and only if both conjuncts are true (at world w). A disjunction is true (at world w) if and only if either disjunct is true (at world w). A negation is true (at world w) if and only if the negand is not true (at world w). The only innovation comes with our new connectives, $\Box$ and $\to$:

- $w \Vdash \Box A$ if and only if for every v in W, $v \Vdash A$.
- $w \Vdash A \to B$ if and only if for every v in W, either $v \nVdash A$ or $v \Vdash B$.

The connective $\Box$ models necessity. A formula $\Box A$ is true if and only if A is true in every world in the evaluation. This makes the conditional robust. A conditional $A \to B$ is true in a world now when there is no world where A is true and B is false; or equivalently, if in every world, if A is true, so is B.

Here is an example evaluation. Our set W has *three worlds, w_1, w_2* and *w_3*:

w_1	w_2	w_3
p	p	${\sim}p$
q	${\sim}q$	${\sim}q$

The diagram indicates the atomic formulas true at each world. For example, q is true at w_1 but not at w_2 or w_3. Now, $\Box p$ is false at w_1 (and at every world) since p is not true at every world (it fails at w_3). Similarly, $\Box q$ is false at every world, since q is false at w_2. The material conditional $p \supset q$ is true at w_1, since p and q are both true there. However, it fails at w_2. It follows that $p \to q$ is false at w_1 (and at every world). So, we have

$$w_1 \Vdash q \quad \text{but} \quad w_1 \nVdash p \to q$$

We have a case (w_1) where q is true, but it doesn't follow that $p \to q$ is true. The fact that there is another possibility (w_2) in which p holds but q fails is enough to ensure that the conditional $p \to q$ also fails. Similarly,

$$w_1 \Vdash p \quad \text{but} \quad w_1 \nVdash {\sim}p \to q$$

since we have $w_3 \Vdash {\sim}p$ and $w_3 \nVdash q$. The other paradox of material implication also fails when the material conditional is replaced by the arrow.

We have just constructed a simple modelling for the modal logic called S5 in the literature. The conditional defined is *often* called the *strict* conditional, to differentiate it from the weaker *material* conditional.

To be specific, we will call our modal evaluations S5 evaluations. Given S5 evaluations, we can define an expanded notion of consequence:

> $X \vDash A$ iff for every S5 evaluation, for every world, if every element of X is true at that world, so is A.

For example, with this definition and the evaluation given above, we have shown that

$$p \nvDash q \to p \quad p \nvDash {\sim}p \to q$$

We can also show that

$$\Box A, \Box B \vDash \Box(A \ \& \ B)$$

by reasoning like the following. Take any S5 evaluation you like, and suppose that w is some world in that evaluation, in which $w \Vdash \Box A$ and $w \Vdash \Box B$. We want to show that $w \Vdash \Box(A \ \& \ B)$. To do that, we must check that in every world v in that evaluation, $v \Vdash A \ \& \ B$. Well, since $w \Vdash \Box A$, we have $u \Vdash A$, for any world u, and hence

$v \Vdash A$. Similarly, since $w \Vdash \Box B$, we have $u \Vdash B$, for any world u, and hence $v \Vdash B$. As a result, $v \Vdash A \ \& \ B$, as we wished to show. Therefore, we have $\Box A, \Box B \vDash \Box(A \ \& \ B)$ as desired.

Here is another example. We will show that

$$\Box(p \vee q) \nvDash \Box p \vee \Box q$$

If it is necessary that either p or q, it does not follow that it is necessary that p or that it is necessary that q. To do this, we try to construct a evaluation with a world w where $w \Vdash \Box(p \vee q)$ while $w \nVdash \Box p \vee \Box q$. For this, we need $w \nVdash \Box p$ and $w \nVdash \Box q$. Therefore, there must be some world in which p fails, and some world in which q fails. However, since $w \Vdash \Box(p \vee q)$ in every world, we have either p or q. But this is not hard to arrange. In world w, we have p but not q. In world v, we have q but not p. The evaluation looks like this.

w	v
p	~p
~q	q

This is enough to show that $\Box(p \vee q) \nvDash \Box p \vee \Box q$.

We have seen one example of *relative* evaluations, at which propositions are given truth values *relative* to some context or other. Once we start down this road, a wide range of possibilities open up. *Temporal* logics allow relativisation to *times*. *Spatial* logics allow relativisation to *locations*. Logics of *belief* and *knowledge* allow relativisation to different belief sets. The introduction of evaluations using *worlds* for modal logics has resulted in an explosion of different formal logics for different purposes.

It seems clear that these evaluations do something right when it comes to modelling conditionals. However, as they stand, they leave something to be desired. One problem stems from the tight connection between necessity and the conditional. In our evaluations, we have

$$p \rightarrow q \vDash \Box(p \rightarrow q) \qquad p \rightarrow q \vDash (p \ \& \ r) \rightarrow q$$

If p implies q, it follows that p *must* imply q. This seems too strong. It is true that if I work hard, I enjoy it. It does not follow that things *must* be like that. There are situations in which I work hard and I don't enjoy it, but these situations are reasonably out of the ordinary.

Similarly, if $p \rightarrow q$, it seems that it need not be the case that $(p$ & $r) \rightarrow q$. If I drink coffee, I like the taste. It doesn't follow that if I drink coffee and you put petrol in it, I like the taste.

David Lewis in his *Counterfactuals* [16], gives an analysis of conditionals that attempts to meet these kinds of objections. For Lewis, worlds come ordered by a relation of *similarity*, and a conditional is true here if in similar worlds where the antecedent is true, so is the consequent. So, on this account, you might have $p \rightarrow q$, without $\Box(p \rightarrow q)$. In worlds close to here where p is true, q is also true. It does not follow that in worlds close to anywhere else, if p is true, so is q. Similarly, we can have $p \rightarrow q$ (since the nearby p-worlds are also q-worlds) but not $(p$ & $r) \rightarrow q$. The nearby p & r worlds are further away, and hence not counted in the previous conditional. Therefore q might fail at these worlds.

Relevance

There are problems of relevance that beset even the most sophisticated modal accounts of conditionals. On any account of consequence seen so far, we have

$$p \, \& \sim p \models q \quad p \models q \lor \sim q$$

These are called the paradoxes of entailment. Some people consider these to be paradoxical since, in both cases, the premise has nothing to do with the conclusion.

You must go right back to the definition of validity:

> An argument is valid if and only if whenever the premises are true, so is the conclusion. In other words, it is impossible for the premises to be true while at the same time the conclusion is false.

Well, according to this definition, or at least according to the second part of it, the argument from p & $\sim p$ to q is valid: because it is impossible for p & $\sim p$ to be true while q is false – for p & $\sim p$ can't be true! It's a contradiction. Similarly, the argument from p to $q \vee \sim q$ is 'valid' in this sense, because $q \vee \sim q$ can't be false.

You can see that this definition doesn't give us any connection between the premises of an argument and its conclusion. According to this definition, the premises alone can ensure that an argument is valid! It's no wonder that our techniques make these paradoxes valid.

So, to reject the paradoxes of entailment, you have to use a different definition of validity. You have to say something like this:

> An argument is *relevantly valid* just in the case whenever the premises are true, then *as a result of that* the conclusion is true.

Now this needs a lot of work. (What does 'as a result of that' mean?) But an account like this, if it can be made to make sense, will reject the paradoxes. If p is true then it need not follow *as a result of the truth of* p that $q \vee \sim q$ is true. Similarly, it is hard to see that if p & $\sim p$ were true then, as a result of that, q turns out to be true too. (To be sure, if q were p or $\sim p$, the inference would work, but these are special cases.)

On the other hand, if p is true then, as a result of that, $p \vee q$ is certainly true. Similarly, if p & q is true then, as a result of that, p must be true. The result looks a bit like the logic we've already seen, but it's a bit different.

This general area is called relevant logic, for, according to this analysis, the premises of an argument must be relevant to its conclusion in order to be valid. A lot of work has gone on in this area since the 1950s.

So, that's one sort of difficulty people have had with the formalism we've been studying. It doesn't turn out to be a crucial objection to the formalism – it merely says that there is another interesting sense of 'valid' that the classical story doesn't capture. If this is to be pursued, you must abandon (or at least modify) the equivalence between $X \vDash A$ and $X, \sim A \vDash$.

Further reading

Grice's pioneering 'Logic and conversation' [9] is widely available in Jackson's edited collection *Conditionals* [14]. This collection includes a range of papers that encompass the debate over truth conditions and assertibility conditions for conditionals, as well as modal accounts of the conditional.

Hughes' and Cresswell's *A New Introduction to Modal Logic* [13] and Chellas' *Modal Logic* [3] both provide sure footed introductions to modal logics. Lewis' *On the Plurality of Worlds* [17] is an in-depth analysis of the philosophical issues involved in talk of modal logic. Chapters 3 and 4 of Read's *Thinking about Logic* [21] and Restall's *Introduction to Substructural Logics* [22] give an introduction to the formal and philosophical issues that arise in the study of relevant logics.

Exercises

Basic

{6.1} Verify each of the following:

$$\Box A \ \& \ (A \rightarrow B) \vDash \Box B$$
$$\Box A \ \& \ (A \supset B) \nvDash \Box B$$
$$\sim \Box A \vDash \Box \sim \Box A$$
$$\Box (A \ \& \ \Box B) \vDash \Box (A \ \& \ B)$$
$$\Box A \ \& \sim \Box B \vDash \sim \Box (\sim A \lor B)$$

{6.2} Let $\Diamond$ be possibility. $\Diamond A$ is defined to be $\sim \Box \sim A$, and so $w \Vdash \Diamond A$ if and only if in some world v, $v \Vdash A$. Show that $\Diamond A \ \& \ \Diamond B \nvDash \Diamond (A \ \& \ B)$ and that $\Diamond (A \lor B) \vDash \Diamond A \lor \Diamond B$.

{6.3} Construct an S5 evaluation in which the 'lightbulb and switches' paradox fails. Construct an evaluation that verifies that

$$(p \ \& \ q) \rightarrow r \nvDash (p \rightarrow r) \lor (q \rightarrow r)$$

Use this evaluation to explain what is going on in terms of possible states of the electrical circuitry involved in the lighting. *Hint:* Think of the different worlds as different states of the electrical system.

Advanced

{6.4} A modality is a string of symbols constructed out of ~ and □, such as ~□ and □~□□. Two modalities are equivalent if and only if the results of prefixing them to an atomic formula are equivalent. (For example, □ and □□ are equivalent, because □p and □□p are equivalent.) Show that there are exactly *six* non-equivalent modalities in S5.

{6.5} Write ◇p & ◇~p as *Cp*. You could say that *Cp* means '*p* is contingent'; that is, *p* can be true, and *p* can be false. Are there any interesting logical laws involving *C*? One example might be ⊨ ~*CCp*: it is not contingent that it is contingent that *p*.

> Under the category of Relation
> I place a single maxim, namely 'Be relevant'.
> – H. P. Grice

Note

1 For the mathematically minded, $Pr(q|p)$ is the probability $Pr(p \& q)$ divided by the probability $Pr(p)$, at least in the case where $Pr(p)$ is not equal to zero.

Chapter 7

Natural deduction

Before turning to *Predicate Logic* in the second part of the book, we will look at one more way to present the logic of propositions. A system of natural deduction gives you a way to develop proofs of formulas, from basic proofs that are known to be valid.

Conjunction, disjunction and negation

The rules tell us how to build up complex arguments from *basic* arguments. The basic arguments are simple. They are of the form

$$X \vdash A$$

whenever A is a member of the set X. We write sets of formulas by listing their members. So $A \vdash A$ and $A, B, C \vdash B$ are two examples.

To build up complex arguments from simpler arguments, you use rules telling you how each connective works. We have one kind of rule to show you how to introduce a connective, and another kind of rule to show you how to eliminate a connective once you have it. Here are the rules for conjunction:

$$\frac{X \vdash A \quad Y \vdash B}{X, Y \vdash A \,\&\, B} \,(\&I)$$

$$\frac{X \vdash A \,\&\, B}{X \vdash A} \,(\&E_1) \qquad \frac{X \vdash A \,\&\, B}{X \vdash B} \,(\&E_2)$$

The rules follow directly from the way we use conjunction. The introduction rule (&I) says that if A follows from X, and if B follows from Y too, then the conjunction $A \,\&\, B$ follows from X and Y together. The elimination rules ($\&E_{1,2}$) say that if something entails a conjunction, then it also entails each conjunct.

For implication, we have two rules:

$$\frac{X, A \vdash B}{X \vdash A \supset B} \,(\supset I) \qquad \frac{X \vdash A \supset B \quad Y \vdash A}{X, Y \vdash B} \,(\supset E)$$

These rules are of fundamental importance for natural deduction systems, as they connect the entailment relation ($\vdash$) to implication. The implication introduction rule ($\supset I$) states that if X together with A entails B, then X entails the conditional $A \supset B$.

So, one way to prove a conditional is to *assume* the antecedent, in order to *prove* the consequent. This is enough to prove the conditional. Conversely, the implication elimination rule ($\supset E$) states that if some set X entails $A \supset B$, and another set Y entails A, then applying the information in X (which gives $A \supset B$) to that in Y (which gives A) gives us the consequent B. So, taking X and Y together gives us all we need for B.

Before going on to see how these rules are used in proofs, we will see the rules for disjunction:

$$\frac{X \vdash A}{X \vdash A \vee B} \,(\vee I_1) \qquad \frac{X \vdash B}{X \vdash A \vee B} \,(\vee I_2)$$

$$\frac{X, A \vdash C \quad Y, B \vdash C \quad Y \vdash A \vee B}{X, Y \vdash C} \,(\vee E)$$

The introduction rules are straightforward enough. If A is entailed by X then so is $A \vee B$. Similarly, if B is entailed by X then so is $A \vee B$. The elimination rule is more interesting. If $A \vee B$ follows from Y, if A (with X) gives C, and if B (with X) also gives C, then Y – which gives $A \vee B$ – also gives C (provided you've got both X too). This is a form of argument by cases. If you know that $A \vee B$, and if A gives you C and B gives you C too, then you have C, either way.

Given the rules, we can construct proofs. A proof of $X \vdash A$ is a tree (this time in the usual orientation, with the root at the bottom) with $X \vdash A$ as the root, in which the leaves are axioms, and in which each step is an instance of a rule. Here is an example:

$$
\cfrac{
  \cfrac{
    \cfrac{\dfrac{A \& C \vdash A \& C}{A \& C \vdash A}\,(\&E) \qquad \dfrac{A \supset B \vdash A \supset B}{\,}}{A \supset B, A \& C \vdash B}\,(\supset E)
  }{A \supset B, A \& C \vdash B \vee D}\,(\vee I_1)
}{A \supset B \vdash (A \& C) \supset (B \vee D)}\,(\supset I)
$$

In this proof, each step is indicated with a horizontal line, labelled with the name of the rule used. The leaves are all axioms, as you can see. The proof demonstrates that $A \supset B \vdash (A \& C) \supset (B \vee D)$.

Each step of the proof follows from the previous steps by way of the rules. However, I constructed the proof in reverse. I know that I wanted to prove that $A \supset B \vdash (A \& C) \supset (B \vee D)$. To do this, I knew that I had just to prove $A \supset B, A \& C \vdash B \vee D$. (To prove $X \vdash A \supset B$, assume A with X, and prove B.) Then it is clear that we can prove $A \supset B, A \& C \vdash B$, since $A \& C \vdash A$, and we are done.

We can also present proofs in *list* form, in which each line is either an axiom or follows from earlier elements in the list by way of the rules:

1	$A \supset B \vdash A \supset B$	Ax.
2	$A \supset (B \supset C) \vdash A \supset (B \supset C)$	Ax.
3	$A \vdash A$	Ax.
4	$A \supset (B \supset C), A \vdash B \supset C$	2,3($\supset$E)
5	$A \supset B, A \vdash B$	1,3($\supset$E)
6	$A \supset (B \supset C), A \supset B, A \vdash C$	4,5($\supset$E)
7	$A \supset (B \supset C), A \supset B \vdash A \supset C$	6($\supset$I)
8	$A \supset B \vdash (A \supset (B \supset C)) \supset (A \supset C)$	7($\supset$I)

In this proof, we have annotated each line with an indication of the lines to which it appeals and the rules used in the derivation. This presentation encodes exactly the same information as the tree. It is *often* easier to produce a proof in list form at first, as you can go 'down the page' as opposed to horizontally across it as the proof gets more complex. Also, in a list proof, you can make assumptions that are not used further in the proof, which can be helpful in producing the proof. However, once the proof is produced, representing it as a tree provides a more direct representation of the dependencies between the steps.

Let's see another example to give you some more ideas of how proofs are produced. Let's prove

$$A \supset ((B \,\&\, C) \supset D) \vdash (A \,\&\, C) \supset (B \supset D)$$

To do this, we know that we will have to assume $A \supset ((B \,\&\, C) \supset D)$, and also $A \,\&\, C$ and B to deduce D. But these together will give us D rather simply. By $A \,\&\, C$, we get A, and this gives us $(B \,\&\, C) \supset D$. $A \,\&\, C$ also gives us C and B, which then give $B \,\&\, C$, which then gives D. So, let's wrap this reasoning up in a proof:

1	$A \supset ((B \,\&\, C) \supset D) \vdash A \supset ((B \,\&\, C) \supset D)$	Ax.
2	$A \,\&\, C \vdash A \,\&\, C$	Ax.
3	$B \vdash B$	Ax.
4	$A \,\&\, C \vdash A$	2(&E)
5	$A \supset ((B \,\&\, C) \supset D), A \,\&\, C \vdash (B \,\&\, C) \supset D$	1,4($\supset$E)
6	$A \,\&\, C \vdash C$	2(&E)
7	$A \,\&\, C, B \vdash B \,\&\, C$	3,6(&I)
8	$A \supset ((B \,\&\, C) \supset D), A \,\&\, C, B \vdash D$	5,7($\supset$E)
9	$A \supset ((B \,\&\, C) \supset D), A \,\&\, C \vdash B \supset D$	8($\supset$I)
10	$A \supset ((B \,\&\, C) \supset D) \vdash (A \,\&\, C) \supset (B \supset D)$	9($\supset$I)

This proof explicitly represents the informal reasoning in the paragraph above.

Negation

The rules so far only give us a fragment of our language. We have conjunction, implication and disjunction. To add the negation rules, it is helpful to first add a proposition $\perp$ (called the *falsum*), which is always evaluated as false. This is governed by the simple elimination rule

$$\frac{X \vdash \perp}{X \vdash A} (\perp\text{E})$$

Since $\perp$ is always false, it does not have an introduction rule. Given $\perp$, we can define negation rules simply:

$$\frac{X, A \vdash \perp}{X \vdash {\sim}A} (\sim\text{I}) \qquad \frac{X \vdash {\sim}A \quad Y \vdash A}{X, Y \vdash \perp} (\sim\text{E})$$

If X together with A entails $\perp$ then we know that X and A can't be true together, so if X is true, A is false: that is, $\sim A$ is true. That is the introduction rule for negation. To exploit a negation, if X entails $\sim A$, and if Y entails A, then it follows that X and Y cannot be true together. That is, they jointly entail $\perp$. These rules govern the behaviour of negation. (You might have noticed that these rules just define $\sim A$ as equivalent to $A \supset \perp$. It is instructive to check using truth tables that $\sim A$ and $A \supset \perp$ are equivalent.) These rules allow us to prove a great many of the usual properties of negation. For example, it is simple to prove that a double negation of a formula follows from that formula, $A \vdash \sim\sim A$:

1	$A \vdash A$	Ax.
2	$\sim A \vdash \sim A$	Ax.
3	$A, \sim A \vdash \perp$	1,2($\sim$E)
4	$A \vdash \sim\sim A$	3($\sim$I)

Similarly, the rule of contraposition, $A \supset B \vdash \sim B \supset \sim A$, has a direct proof:

1	$A \supset B \vdash A \supset B$	Ax.
2	$A \vdash A$	Ax.
3	$A \supset B, A \vdash B$	1,2($\supset$E)
4	$\sim B \vdash \sim B$	Ax.
5	$A \supset B, A, \sim B \vdash \bot$	3,4($\sim$E)
6	$A \supset B, \sim B \vdash \sim A$	5($\sim$I)
7	$A \supset B \vdash \sim B \supset \sim A$	6($\supset$I)

However, the rules for negation cannot prove *everything* valid in truth tables. For example, there is no way to prove a formula from its double negation. (It is instructive to *try* to prove $\sim\sim A \vdash A$. Why is it impossible with these rules? Similarly, the converse of contraposition, $\sim B \supset \sim A \vdash A \supset B$ is valid in truth tables, but cannot be proved using the natural deduction rules we have so far.) To give us the *full* power of truth tables, we have an extra rule

$$\frac{X \vdash \sim\sim A}{X \vdash A} \text{ (DNE)}$$

This is called the double negation elimination rule (DNE). With the rule, we get $\sim\sim A \vdash A$ (apply the rule to the axiom $\sim\sim A \vdash \sim\sim A$ and you have your result) and much more. The full power of truth tables is modelled by these rules. As another example, here is a tautology, the *law of the excluded middle*. It is straightforward to show that $A \vee \sim A$ is a tautology in truth tables. It is a great deal more difficult to prove it using our natural deduction system.

1	$A \vdash A$	Ax.
2	$A \vdash A \vee \sim A$	2($\vee$I)
3	$\sim(A \vee \sim A) \vdash \sim(A \vee \sim A)$	Ax.
4	$A, \sim(A \vee \sim A) \vdash \bot$	2,3($\sim$E)
5	$\sim(A \vee \sim A) \vdash \sim A$	4($\sim$I)
6	$\sim(A \vee \sim A) \vdash A \vee \sim A$	5($\vee$I)
7	$\sim(A \vee \sim A) \vdash \bot$	3,6($\sim$E)
8	$\vdash \sim\sim(A \vee \sim A)$	7($\sim$I)
9	$\vdash \sim A \vee \sim A$	8(DNE)

Typically, proofs that require (DNE) are more complex than proofs that do not require it. In general, if you are attempting to prove something that requires the use of (DNE), you should try to prove its double negation first, and then use (DNE) to get the formula desired.

Natural deduction systems provide a different style of proof to that constructed using trees. In a tree for $X \vdash A$, we attempt to see how we could have X and $\sim A$. If there is some consistent way to do this, the argument is not valid. If there is none, the argument is valid. On the other hand, natural deduction systems construct a derivation of A on the basis of X. The resulting derivation is very close to an explicit 'proof' such as you will see in mathematical reasoning. But natural deduction systems have deficiencies. If something is not provable, the natural deduction system does not give you any guidance as to how to show that. Trees give you worthwhile information for both valid and invalid arguments.

We will not pursue these systems of proof theory any further. To find out more about natural deduction, consult some of the readings mentioned below.

Further reading

Lemmon [15] is still the best basic introduction to this form of natural deduction. Prawitz's original account [20] is immensely readable, and goes into the formal properties of normalisation. For a more up-to-date summary of work in natural deduction and other forms of proof theory, consult Troelstra and Schwichtenberg's *Basic Proof Theory* [30].

The system of logic without (DNE) is called *intuitionistic logic*. The philosophical underpinning of intuitionistic logic was developed by L. E. J. Brouwer in the first decades of the twentieth century. For Brouwer, mathematical reasoning was founded in acts of human construction (our intuition). Brouwer did not think that a formal system could capture the notion of mathematical construction, but nevertheless a logic of intuitionism was formalised by Heyting (see *Intuitionism: An Introduction* [11]). The rule (DNE) fails, since $\sim A$ holds when you have a construction showing that A cannot be constructed or proved. This is a refutation of A. Thus $\sim\sim A$ means that you have a demonstration that there cannot be a refutation of A. This does not necessarily give you a positive construction of A. Similarly, you may have neither a refutation of A nor a construction of A, so $A \vee {\sim}A$ fails as well. Intuitionistic logic is important not only in the philosophy of mathematics and the philosophy of language (see the work of Michael Dummett [4], who uses the notion of verification or construction in areas other than mathematics), but also in the study of the computable and the feasible.

These natural deduction systems are easy to modify in order to model *relevant* logics. We modify the rules to reject the axiom X £A, and accept only the instances A £A (the other elements of X might be *irrelevant* to the deduction of A). Then, there is no way to deduce A £ $B \to A$, since the B was not *used* in the deduction of A. It is also possible to make the number or the order of the use of assumptions important. Slaney's article 'A general logic' [28] is a short essay on this approach to logic, and it is taken up and explored in my *Introduction to Substructural Logics* [22].

Exercises

Basic

{7.1} Prove these, not using (DNE):

$$A \supset {\sim}B \vdash B \supset {\sim}A \quad {\sim}{\sim}{\sim}A \vdash {\sim}A \quad {\sim}A \vee {\sim}B \vdash {\sim}(A \& B)$$
$$ {\sim}(A \vee B) \vdash {\sim}A \& {\sim}B \quad A \& {\sim}B \vdash {\sim}(A \supset B)$$

{7.2} Prove these, using (DNE):

$$\vdash ((A \supset B) \supset A) \supset A \quad {\sim}(A \& B) \vdash {\sim}A \vee {\sim}B \quad \vdash A \vee (A \supset B)$$
$$ {\sim}A \supset {\sim}B \vdash B \supset A \quad (A \& B) \supset C \vdash (A \supset C) \vee (B \supset C)$$

Advanced

{7.3} Show that the natural deduction rules without (DNE) (that is, the rules for intuitionistic logic) are sound for the following three-valued truth tables:

p	q	$p\&q$	$p\vee q$	$p\supset q$	$\sim p$
0	0	0	0	1	1
0	n	0	n	1	1
0	1	0	1	1	1
n	0	0	n	0	0
n	n	n	n	1	0
n	1	n	1	1	0
1	0	0	1	0	0
1	n	n	1	n	0
1	1	1	1	1	0

To do this, show that if $X \vdash A$ can be proved by the natural deduction system then $X \models A$ holds in the three-valued table. (For $X \models A$ to hold, we require that in any evaluation in which the premises are assigned 1, so is the conclusion.) Show, then, that none of the argument forms in Exercise 7.2 are provable without (DNE), by showing that they do not hold in these three-valued tables.

{7.4} Show that these three-valued tables are not *complete* for intuitionistic logic. Find an argument that cannot be proved valid in the natural deduction system, but that is valid according to the three-valued tables.

{7.5} Show that the three-valued Łukasiewicz tables are not sound for intuitionistic logic. Find something provable in intuitionistic logic that is not provable in the three-valued Łukasiewicz tables.

> Nothing prevents us from being natural
> so much as the desire
> to appear so.
> – Duc de la Rochefoucauld

PART 2
Predicate logic

Chapter 8

Predicates, names and quantifiers

Propositional logic, which you know well by now, can establish the validity of many argument forms. As such, it is a very useful tool. However, some arguments are obviously valid, and yet cannot be shown to be so by the methods we've used. For example, the argument

All male philosophers have beards.
Socrates is a male philosopher.
Therefore, Socrates has a beard.

is valid. If all male philosophers have beards, and if Socrates is a male philosopher, then it follows that he has a beard. If Socrates does not have a beard, then either he isn't a male philosopher or he is a counterexample to the claim that all male philosophers have beards. So, if the conclusion is false, one of the premises is false.

However, the most descriptive *propositional* form of this argument is just '*p, q*, therefore *r*', which is as invalid as any argument form can be. We require some new methods to expose the structure of these sorts of arguments. We want a language that will show that this argument has a form. The right kind of form might be something like *this*:

> All *F*s are *G*s.
> *a* is an *F*.
> Therefore, *a* is a *G*.

This form is *valid*. We would like to extend our language in such a way as to make forms like these available. There is a way of doing this, and the resulting language is called the *predicate calculus*. The logic is called *predicate logic*, or sometimes *first-order* logic. The rest of this chapter will involve putting together the language. Only after this will we be able to use it to discover valid argument forms.

Names and predicates

If our language is going to uncover a form responsible for the validity of our argument involving Socrates, it must do two things. It has to be able to name things (such as Socrates) and it has to be able to describe them (such as saying that he has a beard). We will take these one at a time. We start with *names*.

In a language such as English, a proper name is a simple expression that serves to pick out an individual thing. For example 'five', 'India' and 'Richard Nixon' are all proper names. They name a number, a country and a past president of the USA respectively. (Note that I used quotation marks to help name the names. India is a country, but 'India' is not a country. It is a name for a country. Similarly, five is a number, but 'five' is a name of a number.) We will use the letters '*a*', '*b*', '*c*', ..., for proper names in our language of argument forms. We also call proper names simply *names* or *constants* in the rest of this book. (Since we are now using these letters for names, we must set aside some letters for atomic propositions. We will use letters from *a* to *o* to stand for objects, and if this is not enough, we subscript them with numbers, such as b_{23}, c_{3088} and so on. For atomic propositions, we will now use *p, q* and *r*, together with these letters subscripted by numbers.)

PREDICATES, NAMES AND QUANTIFIERS

Next, we must have a way to describe the things we have named. We use predicates to do this. Basically, a predicate is an expression that results in a sentence when a number of names are inserted in the appropriate places. For example,

... is a multiple of ten ...   ... is slightly mad   ... is taller than ...
... is a multiple of ...   ... loves ...   ... is between ... and ...

are all predicates. The first and second of these examples use one name to make a sentence, so they are called *monadic*. The third, fourth and fifth use two names, and are *dyadic*. The last predicate 'is between' requires three names, and is *triadic*. We will use upper-case letters such as '*F*', '*G*' and so on as predicate letters.

You can think of names as naming objects, and predicates as ascribing properties and relations. A name such as *a* names an object (a person, a number, a country, or whatever else), a monadic predicate such as *F* ascribes a property (such as the property of being mad, or being a multiple of ten, or the property of being fun to visit, or whatever else), a dyadic predicate such as *G* ascribes a two-place relation (such as loving, being bigger than, being next to, and whatever else), triadic predicates ascribe three place relations, and so on.

With this up our sleeve, we can form simple propositions combining names and predicates:

India is big	*Bi*
John loves Mary	*Ljm*
John and Mary love each other	*Ljm & Lmj*
John and Mary love themselves	*Ljj & Lmm*
Mary's love for John is not reciprocated	*Lmj & ~Ljm*
If Mary loves John, John doesn't love Mary	*Lmj ⊃ ~Ljm*

Note that our propositions *Bi*, and *Ljm*, and so on, now have their own structure. The first, predicates 'bigness' of India. The second says that John loves Mary. These expressions are propositions with structure, but their structure is not like the structure of complex propositions, such as conjunctions, disjunctions and negations. The structure is not made by combining propositions. Instead, it is made by mixing predicates and names. That said, however, these

115

complexes are still propositions, and so they can be combined with all the machinery of the previous part of this text. So, we can conjoin, disjoin, negate and conditionalise these propositions to make new ones, as the other examples show.

Quantifiers

In this way, we can describe some more of the structure of the argument about Socrates, male philosophers and having beards. But the first premise – all male philosophers have beards – is not of the *subject–predicate* form. It doesn't talk about any particular male philosopher, but rather all male philosophers. It uses a structure called a *quantifier*. Other examples are

Some male philosophers have beards.   Most logic students are intelligent.
At least seven people have been on the moon.   Quite a few Australians live in poverty.

In each of these sentences, we are talking about a *quantity* of objects – *all, some, most, at least seven* or *quite a few*. In the predicate calculus, we will use *two* quantifiers: the *universal* quantifier, which talks about *all* objects, and the *existential* quantifier, which talks about *at least one* object.

To introduce these quantifiers, we will start with a simple case. Suppose I say there is a male philosopher who has a beard. First, to say Socrates is a male philosopher who has a beard, I say

$$(Ma \ \& \ Pa) \ \& \ Ba$$

where a names Socrates, M is the predicate 'is male', p is the predicate 'is a philosopher', and B is the predicate 'has a beard'. To say Greg is a male philosopher who has a beard, you say

$$(Mb \ \& \ Pb) \ \& \ Bb$$

where b names Greg. To say *someone* is a male philosopher with a beard, you might be tempted to say

$$(Mx \mathbin{\&} Px) \mathbin{\&} Bx$$

where x names *someone*. But it won't do to leave things like this, since I might say there is a male philosopher who has a beard and there is a male philosopher who doesn't have a beard. We cannot say this by saying

$$((Mx \mathbin{\&} Px) \mathbin{\&} Bx) \mathbin{\&} ((Mx \mathbin{\&} Px) \mathbin{\&} {\sim}Bx)$$

because the philosopher with the beard and the philosopher without the beard are different people. We use different names for different 'someones', or we use a technique for indicating where in the formula we can make a choice of who the 'someone' is.

It is difficult to determine when we get to choose the 'someone'. Suppose you say 'someone is a male philosopher with a beard' and that I want to deny it. (Perhaps I think all male philosophers are beardless, for some reason.) What does the following formula say?

$${\sim}((Mx \mathbin{\&} Px) \mathbin{\&} Bx)$$

This is the negation of what you said, but it might not say what I want to say. It could mean

It's not the case that someone is a male philosopher with a beard.

but it could just as well mean

Someone is not a male philosopher with a beard.

which says something much weaker. It all hinges on where the choice of x is made. In the first interpretation, we do the negation first, and I say that no choice can be made for x that makes $(Mx \mathbin{\&} Px) \mathbin{\&} Bx$ true. In the second, I make the choice first, and then I do the negation: so I say that some choice can be made for x that makes ${\sim}((Mx \mathbin{\&} Px) \mathbin{\&} Bx)$ true.

Now we can start to define our language with quantifiers. To do this, we first add to the language a stock of variables x, y, z (subscripted with numbers if we run out, as usual). Then we add an *existential quantifier* $(\exists x)$ for each variable x. This means 'here

117

is where I make the choice for x'. (It is called the existential quantifier as it says there exists an object with the required properties.) I will illustrate this with a few examples:

$$(\exists x)((Mx \ \& \ Px) \ \& \ Bx)$$

means someone is a male philosopher with a beard, while

$$(\exists x)((Mx \ \& \ Px) \ \& \ {\sim}Bx)$$

means someone is a male philosopher without a beard. In both these examples, the quantifier has a wide scope as it determines the behaviour of the whole formula. In many cases, the quantifier can occur inside other connectives:

$$\sim(\exists x)((Mx \ \& \ Px) \ \& \ Bx)$$

This formula says that it is not the case that some male philosopher has a beard. We negate the claim that there is a choice for x that can be made to make $(Mx \ \& \ Px) \ \& \ Bx$ true. This differs from

$$(\exists x)\sim((Mx \ \& \ Px) \ \& \ Bx)$$

which just says that there is some choice for x that makes $\sim((Mx \ \& \ Px) \ \& \ Bx)$ true. Our language has more than one variable because we sometimes must make a choice of one thing, dependent on the choice of another. For example, if I say

Some philosopher knows a lawyer

I can go halfway to formalising this by saying

$$(\exists x)(Px \ \& \ x \text{ knows a lawyer})$$

where Px is x is a philosopher. Now if K is the two-place predicate for 'knows' and L is the one-place predicate for 'is a lawyer', how do we formalise x knows a lawyer? It cannot be

$$(\exists x)(Lx \ \& \ Kxx)$$

as this says 'some lawyer knows him or herself'. We use a new variable to choose the lawyer, as we need to talk about the philosopher and the lawyer at the same time. For x knows a lawyer, we can use

$$(\exists y)(Ly \ \& \ Kxy)$$

as this says 'there is a lawyer that x knows', which comes to the same thing. Putting the whole thing together, we get

$$(\exists x)(px \ \& \ (\exists y)(Ly \ \& \ Kxy))$$

which says some philosopher knows a lawyer, as we wished.

We can use the existential quantifier to do more than just formalise statements asserting the existence of various things. We can also *deny* such statements, and this gives us a way to talk about things in general. For example, when I say $\sim(\exists x)((Mx \ \& \ Px) \ \& \ Bx)$, I say that there isn't a male philosopher with a beard. In other words, *no* male philosophers have beards. Or equivalently, every male philosopher is beardless. We have a way of talking in generality. Any proposition of the form

$$\sim(\exists x)Fx$$

says that not anything has property F. This is equivalent to a proposition saying

Everything doesn't have property F

We write this using a new quantifier

$$(\forall x)\sim Fx$$

which is equivalent to $\sim(\exists x)Fx$. The universal quantifier $(\forall x)Fx$ also marks a point at which a choice for x is made. With an existential quantifier, you say that some choice for x works. With a universal quantifier, you say that *every* choice for x works. So, my

119

claim $\sim(\exists x)((Mx \ \& \ Px) \ \& \ Bx)$, which says that no male philosophers have beards, is equivalent to this claim, using a universal quantifier:

$$(\forall x)\sim((Mx \ \& \ Px) \ \& \ Bx)$$

This says that everything is not a male philosopher with a beard. But we can go further. $\sim((Mx \ \& \ Px) \ \& \ Bx)$ is equivalent to $(Mx \ \& \ Px) \supset \sim Bx$, so our claim can be formalised like this:

$$(\forall x)((Mx \ \& \ Px) \supset \sim Bx)$$

This says that for any choice for x, if x is a male philosopher then x doesn't have a beard. This means that no male philosophers have beards, which is what we said the first time.

To sum up: We have added two things to our language. First, *variables* such as x, y and z and *quantifiers* $(\exists x)$, $(\forall y)$, to represent both points in formulas at which instances can be chosen for variables and the *kinds* of choices that are made. These, together with *names* and *predicates*, form the heart of the predicate calculus. Our *language* looks like this:

- p, q, r, p_1, q_2, r_3, etc., ... are atomic *formulas*.
- x, y, z, x_1, y_2, z_3, etc., ... are *variables*.
- a, b, c, a_1, b_2, c_3, etc., ... are *names*.
- Capital letters such as F, G and H are predicates. For each predicate, there is a *number* that tells us the *arity* of the predicate. *Monadic* predicates have arity 1, *dyadic* predicates have arity 2, and so on.
- If F is a predicate of arity n, and $a_1, \ldots, a_n$ are names, then $F \, a_1 \cdots a_n$ is a *formula*.
- If A is a *formula* then so is $\sim A$.
- If A and B are formulas then $(A \ \& \ B)$, $(A \lor B)$, $(A \supset B)$ and $(A \equiv B)$.
- Given a formula A and name a, and any variable x, we will call the result of replacing all occurrences of a in A by x: '$A(a := x)$'. (This is *not* a formula, but it is on the way to becoming a formula. It needs an instruction to tell you how to treat the free variable x.)

- If A is a formula, if a is a name and if x is a variable then $(\exists x)A(a := x)$ and $(\forall x)A(a := x)$ are both *formulas*.

The *scope* of the quantifier $(\exists x)$ in the formula $(\exists x)A(a := x)$ is the displayed instance $A(a := x)$. Similarly, the scope of the quantifier $(\forall x)$ in the formula $(\forall x)A(a := x)$ is the displayed instance $A(a := x)$.

Here is how the rules are used in generating a fomula. Let's take F to be a monadic predicate and G a dyadic predicate. Then $(Fa \ \& \ Gab)$ is a formula. So, replacing the a in this formula by x (so this is $(Fa \ \& \ Gab)(a := x))$, we get $(Fx \ \& \ Gxb)$. Note that this is *not* a formula, because it contains the variable x without any corresponding quantifier. To get a formula, we *bind* that x with a quantifier. I'll choose an existential quantifier, and we get the formula $(\exists x)(Fx \ \& \ Gxb)$. The *scope* of the quantifier $(\exists x)$ in this formula is $(Fx \ \& \ Gxb)$.

In the way that we have defined the language, $(Fx \ \& \ Gxb)$ is not a formula. The only way that variables enter our language is under the scope of a quantifier. A variable outside the scope of a quantifier is said to be *free*. Inside the scope of a quantifier, it is *bound*.

Translation

It is important to be able to translate *to* and *from* the predicate calculus. The first thing to do is to discover the names and predicates used in the English text. For example, say we wish to formalise this argument:

Everyone loves something.
If you love something you think about it.
Therefore everyone thinks about something.

Here there are three *predicates*. We will use the one-place P for 'is a person', L is two-place, and stands for 'loves'. *Lxy* will be read 'x loves y'. And T is also two-place, for 'thinks about'. To formalise the argument, we'll take each proposition one-by-one. The first says *everyone loves something*. 'Everyone' means 'every *person*', and that's a *universally* quantified claim. Everyone loves something is

$$(\forall x)(Px \supset x \text{ loves something})$$

If you choose any object at all, *if* it is a person, *then* it loves something. Now to say that x loves something, we say

$$(\exists y)Lxy$$

We can choose something (call it y) such that x loves it. We used a different variable to talk about this thing, as we must talk about it and the person at the same time. So, everyone loves something is

$$(\forall x)(Px \supset (\exists y)Lxy)$$

Similarly, everyone thinks about something can be translated as

$$(\forall x)(Px \supset (\exists y)Txy)$$

This can be read as follows. Choose anything at all. If it is a person then there is something that this person thinks about. That translates everyone thinks about something suitably well. Finally, we have: If you love something you think about it. This is a harder sentence to translate, since it does not wear its form so explicitly.

To translate it, think about the claim it makes. It is stating a general rule. If you (or anyone) love something, you think about it. It applies to any person, and to any thing they think about. So, you can choose the person and the thing first. The condition is that the person loves the thing:

$$(\forall x)(\forall y)((Px \ \& \ Lxy) \supset \cdots)$$

If you choose x and y, and x is a person and x loves y, then $\cdots$ and the rest says that the person x thinks about the thing y. So we can fill in the gap:

$$(\forall x)(\forall y)((Px \ \& \ Lxy) \supset Txy)$$

It is important to realise that when we say 'something', sometimes it is an existential quantifier (I like *something*) and sometimes it is a universal quantifier (If I like *something*, I think about *it*). To tell what sort of quantifier is used, you have to think about what sorts of choices are being made.

Table 8.1 gives are some more examples of English sentences and their translations into the predicate calculus.

Table 8.1 **English sentences and their translations into the predicate calculus**

English	Predicate calculus
All dogs are mammals	$(\forall x)(Dx \supset Mx)$
Some cats are mammals	$(\exists x)(Cx \& Mx)$
Max loves everyone	$(\forall x)(Px \supset Lmx)$
Someone loves everyone	$(\exists x)(Px \& (\forall y)(Py \supset Lxy))$
Everyone loves someone	$(\forall x)(Px \supset (\exists y)(Py \& Lxy))$

Summary

The language of the predicate calculus has names to refer to objects, and predicates to represent properties and relations.

- The *existential quantifier* ($\exists$) enables us to talk about things without having names for them. $(\exists x)Fx$ states that there is some object with the property F; $(\exists y)(Gy \& Hy)$ means that there is some object that has both property G and property H.
- The universal quantifier ($\forall$) enables us to form generalisations about objects. $(\forall x)Fx$ states that all objects have property F; $(\forall y)(Gy \supset Hy)$ means that everything that has property G also has property H.

Exercises

Basic

{8.1} Use the dictionary:

$$a = \text{Anthea}; \quad b = \text{Brian};$$
$$Gx = x \text{ is a geologist}; \quad Hx = x \text{ is a hairdresser};$$
$$Px = x \text{ is a person}; \quad Lxy = x \text{ is larger than } y$$

What do the following formulas say, translated into English?

1 Ga
2 $\sim Hb$
3 $Ha \lor Gb$
4 $Ha \,\&\, Hb$
5 $Hb \,\&\, Gb$
6 $\sim Gb$
7 $Gb \supset Hb$
8 Lab
9 $\sim Lba$
10 $(\forall y)(Gy \supset Hy)$
11 $\sim(\forall x)(Gx \supset Hx)$
12 $(\forall x)(Gx \supset \sim Hx)$
13 $(\exists x)(Hx \,\&\, Px)$
14 $(\forall x)(Hx \supset Lxb)$
15 $(\forall x)(Px \supset (\exists y)(Py \,\&\, Lyx))$
16 $(\forall x)(Px \supset (\exists y)(Gy \,\&\, Lyx))$
17 $(\forall x)(Px \supset (\forall y)(Lyx \supset \sim Lyx))$
18 $(\exists y)(Py \,\&\, \sim Gy)$
19 $(\exists x)(Px \,\&\, (\forall y)(Py \supset Lxy))$
20 $(\forall x)(\forall y)(\forall z)(Lxy \supset (Lyz \supset Lxz))$

{8.2} Translate the following sentences (where no-one is 'no person' and someone is 'some person'):

1 Brian is a person.
2 If Brian is a hairdresser then he is not a geologist.
3 If Brian is not a geologist, neither is Anthea.
4 No-one is a geologist.
5 Everyone is a geologist.
6 If anything is a geologist, it is a person.
7 Some geologists are people.
8 Some people are geologists.
9 Some geologists are hairdressers.

10 Some hairdressers are not people.

11 Some non-people are not geologists.

12 Some hairdressers are both geologists and people.

13 If Anthea is a geologist then she is larger than someone.

14 If anything is a geologist, it is larger than some hairdresser.

15 Anything that is both a geologist and a hairdresser is not a person.

16 Some geologists are larger than any hairdresser.

17 Any person is not both a geologist and a hairdresser.

18 Anyone is larger than a geologist.

19 Any geologist is larger than every hairdresser.

20 Any hairdressers larger than a geologist are larger than some hairdresser.

21 At least one geologist is larger than at least one hairdresser.

22 At least one geologist is larger than every hairdresser.

23 Every hairdresser is larger than both Anthea and Brian.

24 If everything larger than Anthea is larger than Brian then Anthea is larger than Brian.

25 If anything larger than Anthea is a geologist then Anthea is larger than any hairdresser.

26 Anthea is larger than a hairdresser only if she is larger than a geologist too.

27 Some people are larger than all hairdressers.

28 Some hairdressers are larger than no geologists.

29 A person is a geologist only if he/she is larger than Brian and not larger than Anthea.

30 Any hairdresser larger than a geologist is larger than every person.

{8.3} In Exercise 8.1, indicate the scope of the quantifiers in the formulas by drawing an arrow from the quantifier to the variables the quantifier binds in its scope.

{8.4} Find forms for these arguments.

1 Brian studies linguistics. Brian belongs to the rock-climber's club. So Brian both studies linguistics and belongs to the rockclimber's club.

2 Someone studies linguistics. Someone belongs to the rockclimber's club. Therefore, someone both studies linguistics and belongs to the rockclimber's club.

3 Every solid is soluble in some liquid or other. Therefore, there is a liquid in which every solid is soluble.

4 Only secretaries and administrators are eligible for the Clean Desk Prize. Ian is eligible for the Clean Desk Prize. Therefore Ian is a secretary and an administrator.

5 Whatever exists is material. Therefore, exactly one of the following two claims is true: (1) nothing is material; (2) some material things are mental, and all mental things are material.

6 There is a man in town who shaves all men in town who do not shave themselves. Therefore there is a man in town who shaves himself.

7 Horses are animals. Therefore, heads of horses are heads of animals.

8 The square root of a perfect square is a natural number. No natural number is a fraction. The square root of a natural number other than a perfect square is not a fraction. Therefore the square root of a natural number is not a fraction.

9 If nobody contributes to Oxfam then there is someone who dies of hunger. Therefore, there is a person who dies of hunger if he or she does not contribute to Oxfam.

10 Charles Dodgson (who wrote *Alice in Wonderland* under the pen-name 'Lewis Carroll') was a logician. This is one of his exercises: Nobody who really appreciates Beethoven fails to keep silence while the Moonlight Sonata is being played. Guinea pigs are hopelessly ignorant of music. No one who is hopelessly ignorant of music ever keeps silence while the Moonlight Sonata is being played. Therefore guinea pigs never really appreciate Beethoven.

Advanced

{8.5} Euclid's *Elements* contain many proofs in geometry and arithmetic. One of them is a proof that there are infinitely many primes. This is a summary: 'If there is a greatest prime then there is a second number [namely, one more than the product of all of the primes] that is greater than the greatest prime, and if this second number is not a prime then [since every number has a prime divisor] there is a third number [a prime divisor of this number] that is a prime number and is greater than the greatest prime. Therefore, there is no greatest prime.' Formalise this argument. (This is not easy, but it can be done, using only the predicates 'is a number', 'is greater than' and 'is prime'. Don't translate the material in square brackets – that is there to give you an idea of what is going on.)

{8.6} There is more than one way to define the language of predicate logic. Sometimes people allow variables not bound by any quantifier to appear in formulas. These are called free variables. Can you think of any reasons why we would allow free variables into our formulas? Can you think of any reasons you might want to avoid free variables in formulas?

> Philosophers never balance between profit and honesty,
> because their decisions are general,
> and neither their passions
> nor imaginations
> are interested in the objects.
> – David Hume

Chapter 9

Models for predicate logic

The language of the predicate calculus is not much use without a way of interpreting formulas in that language. We know how to express things in the language, but we have no way of testing argument forms or finding models to make formulas true or false. It is the task of this chapter to introduce models that enable us to do just that.

Domains and extensions

In the first half of the book, when we didn't worry about predicates, names, variables and quantifiers, evaluations for our propositions were simple. You could find a 'way things could be' by assigning truth values to the atomic propositions.

Now there is more to do. We must interpret each of the names and each of the *predicates*. We must know how to deal with the variables and the quantifiers. Our language is richer and has more structure. It follows that our evaluations have to grow to catch up and do more.

A *model* for the language of predicate calculus is made up of a number of things:

> A model of the predicate calculus has a *domain*. This is a *non-empty* set D of *objects*.

The domain is the collection of objects being discussed. If we are talking about numbers, the domain might be the set $\{0, 1, 2, 3, \ldots\}$ of numbers. If we are talking about the university, it might be the collection of lecturers and students and administrative staff. If we are talking about the whole world, the domain might include *everything*: cabbages and kings, tables and chairs, electrons, and galaxies, economies and symphonies.

Nothing in the language is interpreted *directly* by the domain. Instead, the domain underlies the interpretation of everything in the language. First, we evaluate each of the names in the language:

> In a model, every name a is interpreted by an object $I(a)$ from the domain D.
>
> The object $I(a)$ is said to be the denotation of a, or the interpretation of a.

So, if my domain is the little set

[Descartes, Kant]

of two philosophers, and if my language has two names, a and b, I can have four different interpretations of those names. In one interpretation, I might have

$$I(a) = \text{Descartes} \quad I(b) = \text{Kant}$$

129

So a names Descartes and b names Kant. Or I might use the names the other way around:

$$I(a) = \text{Kant} \quad I(b) = \text{Descartes}$$

Or a and b might name Descartes, leaving Kant without a name in our language:

$$I(a) = \text{Descartes} \quad I(b) = \text{Descartes}$$

This is a permissible interpretation of the names. Nothing dictates that different names should name different objects (people give other people more than one name — think of your different nicknames) or that every object must have a name. There is one remaining interpretation for our language in this domain:

$$I(a) = \text{Kant} \quad I(b) = \text{Kant}$$

That explains how names are interpreted in our domains. Now for predicates. Take the example of the one-place predicate 'is a philosopher'. Formalise it by P. Consider the domain

$$\{\text{Descartes, Kant, Einstein}\}$$

The predicate P divides this domain into two groups: the *philosophers* and the *non-philosophers*. Descartes and Kant are philosophers, while Einstein was not. So, for each person in the domain, you have a truth value 1 or 0, recording if the person is a philosopher or not:

	$I(P)$
Descartes	1
Kant	1
Einstein	0

This table gives you the denotation or interpretation of the predicate P. The predicate P is interpreted by a distribution of truth values to objects in the domain. Had things gone differently – had

Kant decided not to go into philosophy, and had Einstein thought that physics was not for him, we might have had a different distribution of truth values:

	$I(P)$
Descartes	1
Kant	0
Einstein	1

Each such distribution of values to objects is an interpretation, or a *denotation* of a one-place predicate. Each one-place predicate is interpreted in this way.

Now consider two-place predicates, such as '... read things written by ...'. We know that Kant read things written by Descartes, but not vice versa. I don't know who Einstein read, but perhaps he read things written by Descartes and not Kant. Each person here read things they wrote themselves. But neither Kant nor Descartes read anything written by Einstein. So, to interpret the two-place predicate R, we have a table:

$I(R)$	Descartes	Kant	Einstein
Descartes	1	0	0
Kant	1	1	0
Einstein	1	0	1

You read the table by looking at the values at the intersections of *rows* and *columns*. To check whether *Kant* read any *Descartes*, you look at the intersection of the Kant *row* with the Descartes *column*. The value is 1, so, according to this table, Kant read Descartes. So, in general, two-place predicates are interpreted by assigning truth values to *ordered pairs* of objects. The order in the pair counts. The issue of whether Descartes read Einstein is very different to the issue of whether Einstein read Descartes.

Three-place predicates are interpreted by assignments of truth values to *ordered triples* of objects. One three-place predicate is '... prefers ... to ...' These are harder to represent on the page, for obvious reasons, so I will not give you any examples in table form.

We will not see many three-place predicates, so this is no great loss. If we wish to interpret a five-place predicate, we call an ordered list of five things a 5-tuple. In general, an ordered list of n things is called an n-tuple. We move now to our general rule for interpreting predicates:

> Each n-ary predicate F is interpreted by an assignment of truth values to all ordered n-tuples from the domain D.

To test out these ideas, let's look at one simple model. Our language has two names, a and b, one monadic predicate, P, and a dyadic predicate, R. The domain has three objects, d, k and e (which are shorthand for the longer names of these people). We interpret the names and predicates like this:

$$I(a) = d$$

$$D = \{d, k, e\} \qquad I(b) = k$$

	$I(P)$
d	1
k	1
e	0

$I(R)$	d	k	e
d	1	0	0
k	1	1	0
e	1	0	1

What propositions can we make in this language? Here is a simple one:

$$Pa$$

That proposition says that the person named by a has the property picked out by P. Who is the person named by a? It's d (Descartes). The property picked out by P is represented in the $I(P)$ table. Here, the d row contains a 1, so the person named out by a has the property picked out by P. Pa is true.

A similar line of reasoning shows that Pb is true too. Therefore, the formulas

$$\sim Pb \quad Pa \equiv Pb \quad Pa \supset \sim Pb$$

are false true and false, respectively. We can evaluate formulas using the logical connectives in the usual way.

Two-place predicates work in just the same sort of way. The formula

$$Rab$$

is false, since the $\langle d, k \rangle$ entry in the table contains a zero. The formulas

$$Rba \quad Rab \vee Rba \quad Rab \equiv {\sim}Rba$$

all come out as true under this interpretation, as you can check for yourself. This gives us some general rules for determining truth in a model:

- $Fa_1 \cdots a_n$ is true iff $I(F)$ assigns 1 to $\langle I(a_1), \cdots, I(a_n) \rangle$.
- ${\sim}A$ is true iff A is not true.
- $A \& B$ is true iff A is true and B is true.
- $A \vee B$ is true iff A is true or B is true.
- $A \supset B$ is true iff A is not true or B is true.
- $A \equiv B$ is true iff either A and B are both true, or A and B are both false.

These rules collect together what we already know.

Quantifiers

In our language, 'everyone reads Descartes' is formalised as

$$(\forall x)Rxa$$

and this is true in our model, for every object is paired with d by the relation $I(R)$. (Look at the d column in the $I(R)$ table.) However, explaining this fact in general is hard. In general, the truth of a complex formula depends on the truth of the formulas used to construct it. What formulas are used to construct $(\forall x)Rxa$? Some instances of this are

$$Raa \quad Rba$$

which say Descartes reads Descartes and Kant reads Descartes. But there is no way to say Einstein reads Descartes in our language, since we have no way of naming Einstein.

The easiest way to remedy this situation is to add a name for Einstein. We already have a perfectly good name for Einstein: 'e' is used in describing the domain. We will therefore use 'e' as the name in our language. In fact, whenever we have a domain such as

$$\{d, k, e\}$$

we will add to the language a new name for each object in the domain (that way, we are always sure to have a name for each object, no matter what other names the language has):

$$d \quad k \quad e$$

We will write the domain elements in sans serif and their names in italics. For writing on paper, you can write the domain elements with underlines, like this: $\{\underline{d}, \underline{k}, \underline{e}\}$. The new names we add for each domain element will be called their standard names. The standard name for a domain element always denotes that domain element. For example, $I(k) = k$ and $I(e) = e$. Then, to test a quantified formula, such as $(\forall x)Rxa$, you check every instance of the formula. An instance is found by taking away the quantifier, and replacing every variable bound by that quantifier (here an x) by a standard name. The instances of $(\forall x)Rxa$ are

$$Rda \quad Rka \quad Rea$$

Here, every instance is true. Therefore, the universally quantified formula is true. Let's look at a slightly more complex proposition: If you read Kant, you're a philosopher. This is formalised as

$$(\forall x)(Rxb \supset Px)$$

How do you evaluate this? The universal quantifier says $Rxb \supset Px$ holds for any object in the domain. So, it is true iff each of

$$Rdb \supset Pd \quad Rkb \supset Pk \quad Reb \supset Pe$$

134

are true. And, you can check that they are. The only false instance of Px is Pe, and in this case, Reb is false too (Einstein doesn't read Kant), so each instance of $Rxb \supset Px$ is true, and so the universally quantified formula is true.

Here are the general rules for evaluating quantified formulas. We have already seen the universal quantifier rule, and the existential quantifier rule is similar.

- $(\forall x)A$ is true iff $A(x := a)$ is true for each a in the domain D.
- $(\exists x)A$ is true iff $A(x := a)$ is true for some a in the domain D.

A universally quantified formula is true just when every instance is true. An existentially quantified formula is true just when some instance is true.

The final nuance in these rules involves being clear on how instances are formed. I have said that the instances of a quantified formula such as $(\exists x)A$ are to be found by stripping the formula of the quantifier and replacing x by a name: you end up with $A(x := a)$. This is true, but only some instances of x in A have to be replaced.

You must replace only those instances that are bound by the outside quantifier in $(\exists x)A$. Here is an example. Take the following formula:

$$(\exists x)(Fx \vee {\sim}(\forall x)Fx)$$

One of its instances is $Fa \vee {\sim}(\forall x)Fx$, but the formula $Fb \vee {\sim}(\forall x)Fb$ is not an instance, as the second Fx in the original formula is bound by the inside universal quantifier, and not the outside existential quantifier.

We will wrap up this section with one more example, of a more complex formula:

$$(\forall x)(Rxa \supset (\exists y)(Py \mathbin{\&} Ryx))$$

This says that if you read Descartes then there's a philosopher who reads you. This is a formula with nested quantifiers. The quantifier $(\exists y)$ is in the scope of the outer quantifier, $(\forall x)$. The formula is a universally quantified formula (that is its main operator), so we check its instances first. They are

$$Rda \supset (\exists y)(Py \ \& \ Ryd) \quad Rka \supset (\exists y)(Py \ \& \ Ryk)$$
$$Rea \supset (\exists y)(Py \ \& \ Rye)$$

The first thing to note is that the antecedents of these conditionals are true (everyone reads Descartes). So, for these instances to be true, we want the consequents to be true too. Let's take these one at a time. The first is

$$(\exists y)(Py \ \& \ Ryd)$$

and its instances are

$$Pd \ \& \ Rdd \quad Pk \ \& \ Rkd \quad Pe \ \& \ Red$$

We want at least one instance to be true, and in this case the first two are, so $(\exists y)(Py \ \& \ Ryd)$ is true. The second formula, $(\exists y)(Py \ \& \ Ryk)$ has these instances:

$$Pd \ \& \ Rdk \quad Pk \ \& \ Rkk \quad Pe \ \& \ Rek$$

and in this case the second instance is true, so our formula is true. The last formula is $(\exists y)(Py \ \& \ Rye)$, and its instances are

$$Pd \ \& \ Rde \quad Pk \ \& \ Rke \quad Pe \ \& \ Ree$$

and here no instance is true. The first two instances are false, as Rde and Rke are false (neither Descartes nor Kant read Einstein) and the last instance is false, as Pe is false (Einstein is not a philosopher). So $(\exists y)(Py \ \& \ Rye)$ is false, and, as a result, $Rea \supset (\exists y)(Py \ \& \ Rye)$ is false. This is an instance of our original formula

$$(\forall x)(Rxa \supset (\exists y)(Py \ \& \ Ryx))$$

which is therefore also false.

This explanation of the falsity of $(\forall x)(Rxa \supset (\exists y)(Py \ \& \ Ryx))$ was extremely long-winded. There is a shorter way to do this when the domain is finite. You can translate out the quantifiers, to get a

136

formula equivalent to it, that has no quantifiers at all. The rules are simple:

> In a finite domain, $(\forall x)A$ is equivalent to the conjunction of its instances, and $(\exists x)A$ is equivalent to the disjunction of its instances.

So, take our formula $(\forall x)(Rxa \supset (\exists y)(Py \ \& \ Ryx))$. The conjunction of its instances is the formula

$$(Rda \supset (\exists y)(Py \ \& \ Ryd)) \ \& \ (((Rka \supset (\exists y)(Py \ \& \ Ryk)) \ \& \ (Rea \supset (\exists y)(Py \ \& \ Rye)))$$

(I have bracketed to the right. You could just as well have bracketed the conjunction to the left, or in any order you like. The order of conjunctions does not matter, as they are all equivalent.) This formula contains three existential quantifiers, which become disjunctions, like this:

$$(Rda \supset ((Pd \ \& \ Rdd) \vee ((Pk \ \& \ Rkd) \vee (Pe \ \& \ Red)))) \ \& \ ((Rka \supset ((Pd \ \& \ Rdk) \vee ((Pk \ \& \ Rkk) \vee (Pe \ \& \ Rek)))) \ \& \ (Rea \supset ((Pd \ \& \ Rde) \vee ((Pk \ \& \ Rke) \vee (Pe \ \& \ Ree)))))$$

You can then read off the evaluation the values for each atomic formula, and then use the standard truth-table rules to calculate the value of the whole formula.

Sometimes the 'translation' method does not work. If the domain in question is infinite, there is no way to unpack each quantifier into a corresponding propositional formula. The quantifiers must be evaluated by hand. Here is an example. Suppose I am reasoning about numbers, and my domain is

$$D = \{0, 1, 2, 3, 4, \ldots\}$$

the collection of all finite counting numbers. The dyadic predicate S might be interpreted as 'smaller than'. It has the following table:

$I(R)$	0	1	2	3	4	...
0	0	1	1	1	1	...
1	0	0	1	1	1	...
2	0	0	0	1	1	...
3	0	0	0	0	1	...
4	0	0	0	0	0	...
.	.	.	.	.	.	

I can only write up *some* of the table, but hopefully you get the idea. We use the symbols

$$0\ 1\ 2\ 3\ 4\ \ldots$$

as names for the numbers, instead of letters, as these are perfectly good names in this context. Now, to evaluate the formula

$$(\forall x)S0x$$

we check if every instance of $S0x$ is true. Now this is simple: *not* every instance is true, as $S00$ is one instance that is false. As a result, $(\forall x)S0x$ is false. For a more complex example, take

$$(\forall x)(\exists y)Sxy$$

This is true just when the instances

$$(\exists y)S0y \quad (\exists y)S1y \quad (\exists y)S2y \quad (\exists y)S3y \cdots$$

are all true. That is, where n is any of $0,1,2,\ldots$, the instance

$$(\exists y)Sny$$

must be true. But, for that, some instance of Sny must be true. And that is easy – pick a bigger number than n for y. That ensures that $(\exists y)Sny$ is true, for any n, and so $(\forall x)(\exists y)Sxy$ is true in our model.

For one last example, consider the formula

$$(\forall x)(\forall y)(\forall z)((Sxy \ \& \ Syz) \supset Sxz)$$

This is true if and only if every instance

$$(Slm \ \& \ Smn) \supset Sln$$

is true, for every number l, m and n. (We have processed all three universal quantifiers in one go.) But if you have any three numbers, if the first is smaller than the second, and the second is smaller than the third, the first must be smaller than the third. Therefore, any of these instances must be true, and so is the original formula.

Our definition of truth (or satisfaction) in models gives us exactly the same definition of validity as with propositional logic:

> $X \vDash A$ if and only if every model satisfying each formula in X also satisfies A.

The unfortunate truth with predicate logic is that testing this is *much* more difficult, as there are many more models to check. To show that $X \vDash A$, you must show that there is no model satisfying X, $\sim A$. That means, no model on a domain of size 1, or of size 2, or 3, or 4 ... and once you have exhausted the finite domains, you should check all the infinite ones too.

Constructing models

If I have an argument form, and I want to show that it is invalid, I construct a model in which the premises are true and the conclusion is false. In this section, we will see a simple method to do that. We will first choose how big our domain is, and then see whether we can construct a model using that domain to make the premises true and the conclusion false.

If the domain you choose is a small one, you can construct an interpretation by translating the quantifiers away. For example, to check the argument from $(\forall x)(\exists y)Rxy$ to $(\exists x)(\forall y)Ryx$ in the two-element domain $\{a, b\}$, we introduce standard names a and b for the objects, and we replace the quantifiers in the premise and the conclusion. The premise $(\forall x)(\exists y)Rxy$ becomes

$$(\exists y)Ray \;\&\; (\exists y)Rby$$

which then becomes $(Raa \lor Rab) \;\&\; (Rba \lor Rbb)$. Similarly, the conclusion $(\exists x)(\forall y)Ryx$ becomes

$$(Raa \;\&\; Rba) \lor (Rab \;\&\; Rbb)$$

Now, to find a model (on this domain) in which the premise is true and the conclusion is false, we just work with the equivalent propositional forms. The tree for this argument is presented in Box 9.1. The tree has two open branches. Both open branches contain different ways to make the premise true and the conclusion false. The left open branch gives us

$$\sim Rab \quad Rbb \quad \sim Rba \quad Raa$$

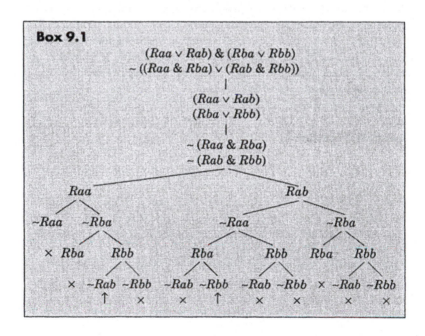

Box 9.1

$$(Raa \lor Rab) \;\&\; (Rba \lor Rbb)$$
$$\sim((Raa \;\&\; Rba) \lor (Rab \;\&\; Rbb))$$

$$(Raa \lor Rab)$$
$$(Rba \lor Rbb)$$

$$\sim(Raa \;\&\; Rba)$$
$$\sim(Rab \;\&\; Rbb)$$

(reading from bottom to top) and the right open branch gives us

$$\sim\!Rbb \quad Rba \quad \sim\!Raa \quad Rab$$

The two branches give us two different models. We take these propositions and use them to give us the interpretations of the two-place predicate R. We get two different tables for $I(R)$. The left branch gives us the first interpretation and the right branch gives us the second.

$I(R)$	a	b
a	1	0
b	0	1

$I(R)$	a	b
a	0	1
b	1	0

Both tables give us models satisfying the premise but not the conclusion. Translating out a formula is quite tedious, especially when you have a moderately large number of names. (Actually, anything over two seems to be tedious enough.) Another way to test an argument in a fixed domain size is by way of trees. You can add some simple tree rules for each quantifier, using the assumption that the domain has a given size.

Existential

To resolve a formula of the form $(\exists x)A$, extend every open branch in which the formula occurs with new branches, each containing an instance of $(\exists x)A$. In the case with a domain with three objects, $\{a, b, c\}$ we have

$$(\exists x)A$$

$$A(x := a) \qquad A(x := b) \quad A(x := c)$$

The rationale of this rule is simple. If $(\exists x)A$ is true then some instance of A must be true. We have one branch for each possibility.

Negated existential

To resolve a formula of the form $\sim(\exists x)A$, extend every open branch in which the formula occurs with every negated instance of $(\exists x)A$. In the case with a domain with three objects, $\{a, b, c\}$, we have

$$\sim(\exists x)A$$
$$|$$
$$\sim A(x := a)$$
$$\sim A(x := b)$$
$$\sim A(x := c)$$

The rationale here is similar. If $\sim(\exists x)A$ is true then no instance of A is true, and hence every instance of $\sim A$ is true. The universal rules are similar.

Universal

To resolve a formula of the form $(\forall x)A$, extend every open branch in which the formula occurs by each instance of $(\forall x)A$. In the case with a domain with three objects, $\{a, b, c\}$, we have

$$(\forall x)A$$
$$|$$
$$A(x := a)$$
$$A(x := b)$$
$$A(x := c)$$

Negated universal

To resolve a formula of the form $\sim(\forall x)A$, extend all of the open branches in which the formula occurs with branches for each of the negated instances of $(\forall x)A$. In the case with a domain with three objects, $\{a, b, c\}$ we have

$$\sim(\forall x)A$$

$$\sim A(x := a) \qquad \sim A(x := b) \qquad \sim A(x := c)$$

Let's use these rules in an example, testing the argument from $(\forall x)(Fx \supset Gx)$ and $(\exists x)\sim Gx$ to $(\exists x)\sim Fx$ in a four-element model is presented in Box 9.2. The tree closes, so there is no counter-example to this argument in a domain of size four. (At the end of this tree, I have taken some liberties to make the tree shorter than it would have been had I applied the rules *literally*. Take the branching to $\sim Fb$ and Gb under $\sim Gb$. In this case, we *should* have also included the branches to $\sim Fa$ and Ga that also occurred under $\sim Ga$. After all, these come from processing $Fa \supset Ga$, and, as the rules indicate, one must place the result of processing a formula in *every open branch in which the formula occurs*. In this case, I didn't, because inserting $\sim Fa$ and Ga into other branches would add nothing except complexity. The branches here each close, and $\sim Fa$ and Ga would do nothing to help that. The case would be *very* different if the tree were not to close. If *that* were the case, one would have to apply the rules religiously, at least in a single open branch.)

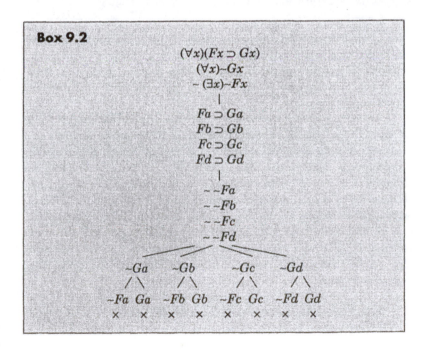

Box 9.2

$(\forall x)(Fx \supset Gx)$
$(\forall x)\sim Gx$
$\sim(\exists x)\sim Fx$

$Fa \supset Ga$
$Fb \supset Gb$
$Fc \supset Gc$
$Fd \supset Gd$

$\sim\sim Fa$
$\sim\sim Fb$
$\sim\sim Fc$
$\sim\sim Fd$

$\sim Ga \quad \sim Gb \quad \sim Gc \quad \sim Gd$
$\sim Fa \; Ga \quad \sim Fb \; Gb \quad \sim Fc \; Gc \quad \sim Fd \; Gd$
× × × × × × × ×

When finite domains suffice

Knowing that there is no counterexample to the argument in a domain of size *four* is reassuring, but it does not tell us that the argument is *valid*. We would have to check domains of other sizes too. In the next chapter, we will introduce tree rules for quantifiers that do not presuppose any particular domain size, and that will give us a method for checking validity of arguments in first-order logic.

To round off this chapter, we will see that there is one case where testing in a finite model suffices for showing that an argument is valid. If your argument is *monadic* (that means that each of the predicates in the argument is monadic) and there are n different predicates in the argument then we can test the argument in a finite domain and be sure that if there is no counterexample in this domain, there is no counterexample at all.

> An argument form containing n monadic predicates is valid iff it has no counterexample in a domain with 2^n elements.

Why is this? This works because each of the n predicates divides the domain up into two classes: those with that property and those without. There are n predicates, so the domain is divided into two pieces n times over, so there are 2^n different sorts of things an object can be.

To be more precise, suppose we have an interpretation I on the domain D that satisfies everything in X, but not the formula A. Call two domain elements a and b in D mates if each predicate in the language assigns the same truth value to both a and b. The domain D is divided into at most 2^n sets of mates. Create a new domain D^* by selecting one element from each set of mates. D^* has at most 2^n elements. For each old element b in D, let its *representative* be the one of its mates that is selected to go into the new domain D^*. We will create a new interpretation I^* on this new domain D^* that satisfies exactly the same formulas as I does. The rules are simple:

- $I^*(F)$ assigns the same value to a that $I(F)$ does.
- If $I(c) = a$ then $I^*(c) = b$, where b is a's representative.

Then, in general, Fa is true (according to I) if and only if Fb is true (according to I^*), where b is the representative of a. It follows that for any formula A, $I(A) = I^*(A)$, so, since we started with a model that was a counterexample to the argument, this *new* model on the domain D^* is also a counterexample, but it now has a domain with no more than 2^n objects. (If the domain D^* has *fewer* than 2^n objects, we may duplicate an object a number of times to make up the numbers to ensure that the domain has *exactly* 2^n objects. A *duplicate* of an object in a model is another object that satisfies exactly the same predicates as the earlier object. Adding duplicates to a model does not affect the truth or falsity of formulas in the model.)

Applying this result in the case of the argument from $(\forall x)(Fx \supset Gx)$ and $(\exists x)\sim Gx$ to $(\exists x)\sim Fx$, we can see that the argument is *valid*, as the tree shows that there is no counterexample in a four-element domain.

Summary

- A model of the predicate calculus has a domain; a non-empty set D of objects.
- In a model, every name a is interpreted by an object $I(a)$ from the domain D.
- Each n-ary predicate F is interpreted by an assignment $I(F)$ of truth values to all ordered n-tuples from the domain D.
- $(\forall x)A$ is true in a model if and only if each of its instances are true. Therefore, in a finite domain, $(\forall x)A$ is equivalent to the *conjunction* of its instances.
- $(\forall x)A$ is true in a model if and only if at least one of its instances is true. Therefore, in a finite domain, $(\forall x)A$ is equivalent to the *disjunction* of its instances.
- $X \vDash A$ if and only if every model satisfying each formula in X also satisfies A.
- An argument form containing n monadic predicates is *valid* iff it has no counterexample in a domain with 2^n elements.

145

Exercises

Basic

{9.1} Given the following model with the domain $D = \{a, b, c\}$:

	I(F)	I(G)
a	0	1
b	1	1
c	1	0

I(T)	a	b	c
a	0	1	0
b	1	0	1
c	0	1	0

$(\forall x)(Rxa \supset (\exists y)(Py \,\&\, Ryx))$
evaluate the following formulas:

1. $(\forall x)(Tx \supset Gx)$
2. $(\forall x)(\forall y)(Txy \supset Tyx)$
3. $(\forall x)(\forall y)(Txy \supset (Tyx \,\&\, {\sim}Fx))$
4. $(\exists x)(\forall y)((Txy \,\&\, Fy) \supset (Gxy \,\&\, Txy))$
5. $(\forall x)(\forall y)((\exists z)(Txz \,\&\, Txy) \supset (\exists z)(Tyz \,\&\, Tzx))$

{9.2} Given the domain

$$D = \{1, 2, 3, \dots\}$$

interpret the predicates S 'smaller than' and D 'divides' as follows:

I(S)	1	2	3	4	...
1	0	1	1	1	...
2	0	0	1	1	...
3	0	0	0	1	...
4	0	0	0	0	...
.	.	.	.	.	

I(D)	1	2	3	4	...
1	1	1	1	1	...
2	0	1	0	1	...
3	0	0	1	0	...
4	0	0	0	1	...
.	.	.	.	.	

(*Dmn* is true if m divides evenly into n.) Which of the following formulas are true?

1 $(\forall x)(D2x \supset D4x)$
2 $(\forall x)(\forall y)(Dxy \vee Dyx)$
3 $(\forall x)(\exists y)(Dxy \,\&\, Dyx)$
4 $(\exists x)(\exists y)(Dxy \,\&\, {\sim}Dyx)$
5 $(\exists x)(\forall y)(Dxy \vee Syx)$
6 $(\exists x)(\forall y)(Syx \supset Dyx)$
7 $(\forall x)(\exists y)(Sxy \,\&\, Dyx)$
8 $(\forall x)(\forall y)(Sxy \supset {\sim}Dyx)$
9 $(\exists x)(\forall y)(Dxy \supset (\exists z)(Szx \,\&\, Dzy))$
10 $(\exists x)(\forall y)Dyx \supset (\forall x)(\forall y)Dxy$

{9.3} Test the following formulas in two-element domains, using any technique you wish. Which are true in each model? Which are false in some? For those that have counterexamples, present a counterexample as a table of values for F and G.

1 $(\forall x)(Fx \supset Gx) \vee (\forall x)(Fx \supset {\sim}Gx)$
2 $(\forall x)(Fx \supset (Gx \vee {\sim}Gx))$
3 $(\exists x)Fx \vee (\exists x){\sim}Fx$
4 $(\forall x)(Fx \vee {\sim}Fx)$
5 $(\forall x)Fx \vee (\forall x){\sim}Fx$
6 $(\forall x)Fx \vee (\exists x){\sim}Fx$
7 $(\forall x)Fx \supset (\exists x)Fx$
8 $(\exists x)(Fx \supset (\forall y)Fy)$
9 $(\forall x)(Fx \supset (\forall y)Fy)$
10 $(\forall x)(Fx \supset (\exists y)Fy)$

{9.4} Test the following arguments in three-element worlds. For any that are not valid, present the counterexample in a table.

1 $(\forall x)(Gx \supset Hx)$, therefore $(\forall x)({\sim}Gx \supset {\sim}Hx)$
2 $(\forall x)Gx \supset (\forall x)Hx$, therefore $(\forall x)(Gx \supset Hx)$
3 $(\forall x)Gx \,\&\, (\forall x)Hx$, therefore $(\forall x)(Gx \,\&\, Hx)$
4 $(\exists x)(Gx \equiv Hx)$, therefore ${\sim}(\forall x)(Gx \supset Hx)$
5 $(\exists x)(Gx \,\&\, Hx)$, therefore $(\exists x)Gx \,\&\, (\exists x)Hx$
6 $(\forall x)(Gx \supset (\forall y)Hy)$, therefore $(\forall x)(Gx \supset Hx)$
7 $(\forall x)(Gx \supset Hx)$, $(\forall x)Gx$, therefore $(\forall x)Hx$

8 $(\forall x)(Gx \supset Hx)$, $(\exists x)Gx$, therefore $(\exists x)Hx$

9 $(\forall x)(Gx \supset {\sim}Hx)$, therefore $(\exists x)(Gx \& {\sim}Hx)$

10 $(\exists x)(Gx \& {\sim}Hx)$, therefore ${\sim}(\forall x)(Gx \supset {\sim}Hx)$

Advanced

{9.5} How many different assignments of names are there from a language with 3 names, into a domain of 4 objects? How many different assignments are there from a language of n names into a domain of m objects?

{9.6} How many different models are there of a 3-place predicate in a domain of 2 objects? How many different models are there of a n-place predicate in a domain of m objects?

{9.7} How many different models are there in a language with n names, m monadic predicates and j dyadic predicates in a domain of k objects?

{9.8} Find a sentence that is satisfied in every finite model, but that is not satisfied in some infinite model. *Hint*: It must feature at least a two-place predicate.

It's a small world after all.
– Walt Disney

Chapter 10

Trees for predicate logic

Working with finite models is tedious – especially when you have three or more predicates, and you have to expand quantifiers with eight constants. And furthermore, the method isn't going to be definitive with arguments containing any predicates of arity greater than 1. So, we need another method to deal with quanti-fiers. There is a method that works – *trees*. When we use trees to evaluate arguments, we construct the model as we go. We don't have to decide in advance how many objects there are in the model. We can 'introduce new objects' as required.

Tree rules for quantifiers

There is a simple extension of trees that can cope with quantifiers. All we need add are extra rules for the quantifiers.

Existential

To resolve a formula of the form $(\exists x)A$, extend any open branch in which the formula occurs with an instance of A using a new name that has not occurred in the branch before.

$$(\exists x)A$$
$$|$$
$$A(x := a) \quad \text{where } a \text{ is } new$$

The rationale of this rule is simple. If $(\exists x)A$ is true then some instance of A must be true. We have no idea *which* object does the job, and we cannot presume we've seen a name for this object already. So, we use a *new* name, and we are safe. If there is a model satisfying $(\exists x)A$ then this model can also satisfy $A(x := a)$, because we can choose the interpretation of the new name a to be an object picked out by A.

Negated existential

Given a formula of the form $\sim(\exists x)A$, you can extend any open branch in which the formula occurs by any instance of A, for *any* name you wish.

$$\sim(\exists x)A$$
$$|$$
$$\sim A(x := a) \quad \text{for any name } a$$

The rationale here is similar. If $\sim(\exists x)A$ is true then *nothing* is truly described by A, and hence everything is $\sim A$. I can't assume I have *all* of the names at my disposal when I get to work with the formula $\sim(\exists x)A$, so *whenever* a new name is added to the branch, I can add a new instance of $\sim A$ to that branch.

The universal rule works on the same principle.

Universal

Given a formula of the form $(\forall x)A$, you can extend any open branch in which the formula occurs by any instance of A, for any name you wish:

$$(\forall x)A$$
$$|$$
$$A(x := a) \quad \text{for any name } a$$

The negated universal rule is just like the existential rule:

Negated universal

To resolve a formula of the form $\sim(\forall x)A$, extend any open branch in which the formula occurs with an instance of $\sim A$ using a new name that has not yet occurred in the branch.

$$\sim(\forall x)A$$
$$|$$
$$\sim A(x := a) \quad \text{where } a \text{ is } new$$

As you can see, the rules come in two different kinds. We will call the *existential* quantifier rule and the *negated universal* quantifier rule *particular* rules. You use them *once* only. They introduce a new name to the tree, for a particular object.

In the same vein, we will call the *universal* quantifier rule and the *negated existential* rule *general* rules. These rules can be used *repeatedly*. You are allowed to form instances of $(\forall x)A$ and $\sim(\exists x)A$ as *often* as you like. They apply generally to all objects in the domain.

We will treat general rules and particular rules differently when creating trees, much in the same way as treating branching rules differently to linear rules.

Let's use the rules to test an argument. We will test the argument from $(\forall x)(Fx \supset Gx)$ and $(\exists x)\sim Gx$ to $(\exists x)\sim Fx$. As before, you start the tree with the premises and the negated conclusion. Here is the top of the tree as we start:

151

$$(\forall x)(Fx \supset Gx)$$
$$(\exists x){\sim}Gx$$
$${\sim}(\exists x){\sim}Fx$$

These three formulas are all complex, so we have a choice of rules to apply. General rules apply to the first formula $(\forall x)(Fx \supset Gx)$, and the last formula ${\sim}(\exists x){\sim}Fx$, and a particular rule applies to the middle formula $(\exists x){\sim}Gx$.

We will apply the particular rule first, as it will give us a name to use to substitute into the other universal rules we will use later. So, we resolve the existential quantifier, using a name new to the branch. The name a hasn't been used yet, so we make the substitution and extend the branch as follows:

$$(\forall x)(Fx \supset Gx)$$
$$(\exists x){\sim}Gx \quad \checkmark a$$
$${\sim}(\exists x){\sim}Fx$$
$$|$$
$${\sim}Ga$$

Once we extended the tree with ${\sim}Ga$, we ticked the original formula $(\exists x){\sim}Gx$ off, to indicate that we have exhausted its content. We have placed an a after the tick to indicate that we have resolved the formula by substituting the name a. This reminds us that we cannot use a to resolve any other particular rules, as a is now in the branch.

On the other hand, we can substitute a in general rules, as these apply to every object in the domain. In fact, that is what we will do now. We have a at our disposal, so we will substitute it into the universal quantifier at the top of the tree:

$$(\forall x)(Fx \supset Gx)\backslash a$$
$$(\exists x){\sim}Gx \quad \checkmark a$$
$${\sim}(\exists x){\sim}Fx$$
$$|$$
$${\sim}Ga$$
$$|$$
$$Fa \supset Ga$$

We indicate that we have substituted a into the formula at the top of the tree by writing '$\backslash a$' after the formula. This reminds us that we no longer have to substitute a into this formula. For our next move, let's substitute a into the negated existential formula $\sim(\exists x)\sim Fx$:

$$(\forall x)(Fx \supset Gx) \quad \backslash a$$
$$(\exists x)\sim Gx \quad \checkmark a$$
$$\sim(\exists x)\sim Fx \quad \backslash a$$
$$|$$
$$\sim Ga$$
$$|$$
$$Fa \supset Ga$$
$$|$$
$$\sim\sim Fa$$

We get the formula $\sim\sim Fa$, and we write '$\backslash a$' on the third line to indicate that we have substituted the a on this line. Now, we could process $\sim\sim Fa$, but that would be a waste of time, as we can get a closure immediately by resolving the conditional $Fa \supset Ga$:

$$(\forall x)(Fx \supset Gx) \quad \backslash a$$
$$(\exists x)\sim Gx \quad \checkmark a$$
$$\sim(\exists x)\sim Fx \quad \backslash a$$
$$|$$
$$\sim Ga$$
$$|$$
$$Fa \supset Ga \quad \checkmark$$
$$|$$
$$\sim\sim Fa$$

$$\sim Fa \qquad Ga$$
$$\times \qquad \times$$

So, the tree closes, and the argument form is *valid*. The reasoning is perfectly general, as it applies in *any* model. The tree tells us that if $(\exists x)\sim Gx$ is true, there must be some object with the property $\sim G$. Call the object a. Now, since $Fx \supset Gx$ holds of every object, it holds of a, so we have $Fa \supset Ga$. And we want to try to make $\sim(\exists x)\sim Fx$ true, so we must make $\sim\sim Fa$ true too. These three requirements are inconsistent, so there is no way to make the three formulas true, in any model, on a domain of any size. The reasoning works no matter how large the domain.

This tree is much simpler than the tree used in the previous chapter to test the argument in a three-element model. Our tree is smaller, and it is more general. It shows that the argument has no counterexample in any model.

Let's use the rules to show that $(\forall x)(Fx \supset (\exists y)Fy)$ is a tautology. That means, it is true in *every* model, no matter how large or small. To show that this must be the case, we try to find a model in which it is false. The tree is simple:

$$\sim(\forall x)(Fx \supset (\exists y)Fy) \quad \checkmark\ a$$
$$|$$
$$\sim(Fa \supset (\exists y)Fy) \quad \checkmark$$
$$|$$
$$Fa$$
$$\sim(\exists y)Fy \quad \backslash a$$
$$|$$
$$\sim Fa$$
$$\times$$

The first step was to apply the particular rule to the negated universal quantifier. This gave us a new name a, and we learned that $\sim(Fa \supset (\exists y)Fy)$ must be true. This is a negated conditional, so, to make that true, Fa and $\sim(\exists y)Fy$ must be true. But this negated existential is inconsistent with what we already know! We have Fa, but substituting a into $\sim(\exists y)Fy$ gives us $\sim Fa$, a contradiction. Therefore this formula is true in every model. So we know that it is a tautology. This is fortunate, because the formula *ought* to be a tautology. It says that for anything you care to choose, if *it's* got property F then *something* has property F. That sounds like the kind of thing that ought to be true in every model.

When trees don't close

Let's look at a tree that doesn't close. The tree for $(\exists x)Fx \,\&\, (\exists x)Gx$ $\nvdash (\exists x)(Fx \,\&\, Gx)$ is presented in Box 10.1. This tree does not close:

Box 10.1

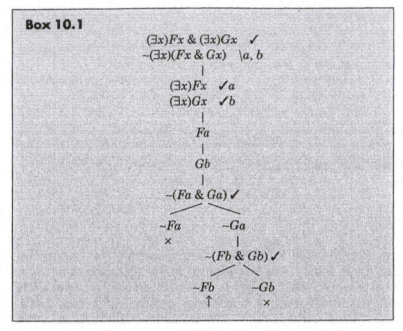

the middle branch is open. Furthermore, the middle branch is *complete*, in the sense of the following definition:

> An open branch in a tree is *complete* iff every resolvable formula has been resolved, and every name in the branch has been substituted into every general formula in the branch. (Furthermore, *some* name has been substituted into each general formula in the branch.)

What does this mean? One way of thinking about it is this: a *complete* open branch in a tree is a world unto itself. For every existentially quantified formula $(\exists x)A$ in the branch, there is a (named) object a occuring in the branch such that $A(x := a)$ is in the branch. Similarly, for every universally quantified formula $(\forall x)A$ in the branch, and for every name a in the branch, the formula $A(x := a)$ is also in the branch. This branch describes a coherent, consistent and complete possibility, requiring nothing *else* to make everything in that branch true.

In our example tree, the only general formula is ~(∃x)(Fx & Gx), and this has had both names a and b substituted into it. (The extra condition in parentheses has been added to deal with a special case that comes up next. Ignore it for the moment.)

The middle branch in our tree is complete. So, we will read off the atomic formulas in that branch to create a model. The names are a and b, so we will make our domain D = {a, b}. The interpretation for F and G is read off the branch by looking at the atomic formulas. The branch contains Fa and ~Fb, ~Ga and Gb. This tells us that our interpretation for F and G looks like this:

	$I(F)$	$I(G)$
a	1	0
b	0	1

This interpretation suffices to make the premise of the argument true (there is an F and there is a G) but to make the conclusion false (there is no object which is both an F and a G). So, trees work with predicate logic in just the same way as with propositional logic. Closed trees give you valid arguments, and complete open branches give you counterexamples.

The parallel with propositional logic is not perfect, however. Sometimes your tree will *never* stop. The rules just make you keep going and going and going. What should you do in these sorts of situations? Let's see an example.

Is the formula (∀x)(∃y)Lxy satisfiable? We will check this by creating a tree for it. The tree is given here:

$$(\forall x)(\exists y)Lxy \quad \backslash a,b,c$$
$$|$$
$$(\exists y)Lay \checkmark b$$
$$|$$
$$Lab$$
$$|$$
$$(\exists y)Lby \checkmark c$$
$$|$$
$$Lbc$$
$$|$$
$$(\exists y)Lcy \checkmark d$$
$$|$$
$$Lcd$$
$$\cdot$$
$$\cdot$$
$$\cdot$$

The first interesting thing about this tree is that we had to invent a name to substitute into the universal quantifier at the top of the tree to get the tree going. This is permissible, as we know that any domain must have at least one object. So, we can give that object a name (here it is a) and continue from there. This happens in general: if you have a general formula in a branch, the branch is not completed until you have substituted at least one name into the formula.

The next striking thing about this tree is the fact that it goes on forever. Any completed branch (and this tree will only ever have one branch) must be infinite. The infinite branch given by completing the tree is reasonably simple to understand. It helps if we use different names instead of a, b, c, ..., as we will use infinitely many names. If we use different names, a_1, a_2, a_3, a_4, etc., you can see that the branch will contain each of these formulas:

$$La_1a_2 \ La_2a_3 \ La_3a_4 \ \ldots \ La_n \, a_{n+1} \ \ldots$$

The name a_1 is the first to be substituted into $(\forall x)(\exists y)Lxy$. Then, given $(\exists y)La_1y$, we get a new name, a_2. This goes back into the universal quantifier, to give us $(\exists y)La_2y$, and the process repeats ..., which eventually gives us a_n, and $(\exists y)La_ny$, and hence a new name a_{n+1}, which goes back into the universal quantifier, and the process continues ad infinitum.

We can summarise the information contained in the tree in a table like this:

$I(L)$	a_1	a_2	a_3	$\cdots$
a_1		1		
a_2			1	
a_3				
.				

The 1s in the table are given by the formulas La_na_{n+1} in the branch. The other entries in the table are left blank, as we are given no information one way or the other about them. It is consistent with this branch to have La_1a_1, and it is also consistent to have $\sim La_1a_1$.

So, this table contains *all* of the information given by the open branch. Any interpretation consistent with that table will make the formula $(\forall x)(\exists y)Lxy$ true. For example, we can construct an interpretation by making all other values false:

$I(L)$	a_1	a_2	a_3	$\cdots$
a_1	0	1	0	
a_2	0	0	1	
a_3	0	0	0	.

This is an interpretation that makes our original formula true. Another interpretation makes all the other values *true*.

$I(L)$	a_1	a_2	a_3	$\cdots$
a_1	1	1	1	
a_2	1	1	1	
a_3	1	1	1	.

This satisfies the original formula equally well. There are even simpler ways of making the formula true. For example, there is no need for the objects $a_1, a_2, a_3, \ldots$ named by the names $a_1, a_2, a_3, \ldots$ to be *different*. In this last interpretation, *each* is related by L to every other object. As far as the interpretation goes, each object a_n is *indistinguishable* from any other, so we may as well have the following one-element interpretation:

$I(L)$	a_1
a_1	1

In general, given a completed branch of a tree, you ought to find the pattern in the branch, and display the information given explicitly in that branch by a table. Then, you can construct any interpretation consistent with that information to satisfy the formulas in that branch. This includes using one object for more than one name in the branch, provided that the information known about the different 'objects' is consistent. We will consider one more example to explain this last constraint. Here we test the consistency of the formula $(\forall x)(\exists y)(Lxy \,\&\, {\sim}Lyx)$. This is very similar to the case we have already seen. The tree for this formula is given below. (This time I have used names a_1, a_2, ... because I knew it would continue forever.)

$$(\forall x)(\exists y)(Lxy \,\&\, {\sim}Lyx) \backslash a_1,\, a_2,\, a_3$$
$$|$$
$$(\exists y)(La_1y \,\&\, {\sim}Lya_2) \checkmark a_2$$
$$|$$
$$La_1a_2 \,\&\, {\sim}La_2a_1$$
$$|$$
$$La_1a_2$$
$${\sim}La_2a_1$$
$$|$$
$$(\exists y)(La_2y \,\&\, {\sim}Lya_2) \checkmark a_3$$
$$|$$
$$La_2a_3 \,\&\, {\sim}La_3a_2$$
$$|$$
$$La_2a_3$$
$${\sim}La_3a_2$$
$$|$$
$$(\exists y)(La_3y \,\&\, {\sim}Lya_3) \checkmark a_4$$
$$|$$
$$La_3a_4 \,\&\, {\sim}La_4a_3$$
$$\cdot$$
$$\cdot$$
$$\cdot$$

This tree also continues indefinitely. A completed branch now contains

$$La_1a_2 \quad {\sim}La_2a_1 \quad La_2a_3 \quad {\sim}La_3a_2 \quad La_3a_4 \quad {\sim}La_4a_3 \quad \cdots \quad La_na_{n+1} \quad {\sim}La_{n+1}a_n$$

In table form, we get this information about any interpretation:

$I(L)$	a_1	a_2	a_3	a_4	...
a_1		1			
a_2	0		1		
a_3		0		1	
a_4			0		
.					

Any interpretation that fills in the blanks in this table will satisfy the formula $(\forall x)(\exists y)(Lxy \ \& \ {\sim}Lyx)$. So, populating the rest of the table with zeros gives us one interpretation:

$I(L)$	a_1	a_2	a_3	a_4	...
a_1	0	1	0	0	
a_2	0	0	1	0	
a_3	0	0	0	1	
a_4	0	0	0	0	
.					

We can still get a *finite* model by noticing that not every name a_n need name a different object. But we have to be careful. We know that a_1 and a_2 must name different objects, since we have La_1a_2 and ${\sim}La_2a_1$. Similarly, a_1 and a_3 name different objects, as La_1a_2 but ${\sim}La_3a_2$; and in general, a_n, a_{n+1} and a_{n+2} must name different objects. This is the only requirement we must satisfy. There is nothing that tells us that a_1 and a_2 must name different objects, or that a_2 and a_5 must. In fact, we can identify every third a_n to get a very compact table:

$I(L)$	a_1	a_2	a_3
a_1	0	1	0
a_2	0	0	1
a_3	1	0	0

This is the smallest domain in which the formula $(\forall x)(\exists y)(Lxy \ \& \ {\sim}Lyx)$ can be satisfied.

Why the tree method works

The tree method works in the following two senses.

Fact 1

If X is satisfiable then, in any totally developed tree for X, some branch remains open. That is, if $X \not\models$ then $X \not\vdash$. This is the soundness theorem. If an inference can be proved valid using trees, it is valid.

Fact 2

If, in some totally developed tree for X, some branch remains open then X is satisfiable. Therefore, if $X \not\vdash$ then $X \not\models$. *This is the completeness theorem. If an inference is valid, it can be proved so using trees.*

These facts are the same as those we proved for propositional logic. They jointly demonstrate that trees for predicate logic are a good match for the models we have defined. Proving these facts is not *much* more difficult than in the propositional case, and I will complete this chapter with demonstrations of both of these facts.

Proof of fact 1

If X is satisfiable, there is some model that makes true every formula in X. We will use I to name the interpretation function of this model, and, for any formula A made up out of the atomic formulas that appear in X, we will write '$I(A)$' for the truth value I assigns to A. Since X is satisfiable, if A is a sentence in X, $I(A) = 1$. If A is the negation of a sentence in X, $I(A) = 0$.

As in the propositional case, we will show that in a completed tree for X, there is some branch in which every formula is satisfied by an interpretation I. It follows that this branch is open, since it can contain no contradictory pair of formulas A and $\sim A$, as they are both satisfied by I. So, if we find such a branch, we are done: our tree contains an open branch.

Finding such a branch is quite simple. You start at the top of the tree, with the formulas in X. These are each satisfied by I, since that is what we assumed. Now, for each rule that is applied to extend the tree, at least one of the branches generated will give us formulas that are satisfied by I, provided that the formula resolved is also satisfied by I. The propositional connectives work in just the same way as before. The only new work is as a result of the quantifiers. Here, we must expand the interpretation as we go along, as we add names to the language. We will now prove that if I satisfies all formulas in a partially completed branch then there is an interpretation I^* that might extend I, which satisfies one of the branches extending the partially completed branch.

If we resolve a existential quantifier $(\exists x)A$ then, since the formula appears in the branch, we know that $I((\exists x)A) = 1$. The rule adds $A(x := a)$ to the branch, where a is a name new to the branch. The name a is not interpreted by I_0, so we extend I to interpret a. We get a new interpretation I_0 that agrees with I on all of the old language, and assigns a to some element in the domain D. What should we choose as $I_0(a)$? We want to make sure that $I_0(A(x := a)) = 1$. This is simple: we know that $I((\exists x)A) = 1$, so there is some object c in the domain A where $I(A(x := c)) = 1$. So, we let $I_0(a) = c$, and this ensures that $I_0(A(x := a)) = 1$ too, as a is interpreted in the same way as c, as naming the object c.

If we resolve a negated universal quantifier $\sim(\forall x)A$ then we have $I((\forall x)A) = 0$. The rule adds $\sim A(x := a)$ to the branch, where a is a name new to the branch. Again, a is not interpreted by I, so we extend I to an interpretation I_0 that also gives a referent to a. We want to make sure that $I_0(\sim A(x := a)) = 1$. This is simple: we know that $I((\forall x)A) = 0$, so there is some object c in the domain A where $I(A(x := c)) = 0$. So, we let $I_0(a) = c$, and this ensures that $I_0(\sim A(x := a)) = 1$ too, as a is interpreted in the same way as c, as naming the object c.

If we apply the rule to a universal quantifier $(\forall x)A$ then, we have $I((\forall x)A) = 1$. The rule adds $A(x := a)$ for any name a we like. Since $I((\forall x)A) = 1$, we know that $I(A(x := a)) = 1$ for any name we like, and hence the added formula $A(x := a)$ is also satisfied by I. There is no need to extend our interpretation I in this case.

If we apply the rule to a negated existential quantifier $\sim(\exists x)A$ then we know that $I((\exists x)A) = 0$. The rule adds $\sim A(x := a)$ for any name a we like. Since $I((\exists x)A) = 0$, we know that $I(A(x := a)) = 0$ for any name we like, and hence the added formula $\sim A(x := a)$ is also satisfied by I. There is no need to extend I in this case either.

So, if the formulas at X at the top of the tree are satisfied by an interpretation I, there is some open branch in the tree that is also satisfied by an interpretation. That interpretation is not necessarily the same as I, as it might be an extension of I, designed to interpret the new names introduced by the particular rules applied in the branch. So, the tree remains open: if $X \not\models$ then $X \not\vdash$.

Proof of fact 2

Suppose a completed branch in a tree for X remains open. We wish to construct an interpretation satisfying X, and everything in that branch. The construction is similar to the propositional case. Take the domain of the interpretation to be the names appearing in the branch. If a is a name in the branch, we interpret a as referring to itself: $I(a) = a$. We fix the interpretations of the predicates similarly.

If $Fa_1 \cdots a_n$ is in the branch, $I(F)$ assigns true to $\langle a_1, \ldots, a_n \rangle$. If $\sim Fa_1 \cdots a_n$ is in the branch, $I(F)$ assigns false to $\langle a_1, \ldots, a_n \rangle$. (Any value can be applied if neither $Fa_1 \cdots a_n$ nor its negation is in the branch.) This is a consistent model as the branch is not closed.

We prove by induction on the formulas in the branch that if A is in the branch, $I(A) = 1$, and if $\sim A$ is in the branch, $I(A) = 0$. The atomic formulas $Fa_1 \cdots a_n$ and $\sim Fa_1 \cdots a_n$ work because I was defined to *make* them work. The propositional connectives work because the situation is unchanged from the propositional case.

For a universal quantifier, if $(\forall x)A$ is in the branch then $A(x := a)$ is in that branch for *every* name a appearing in that branch (the branch is complete). By hypothesis, $I(A(x := a)) = 1$ for each a, so $I((\forall x)A) = 1$ too, by the interpretation rule for the universal quantifier.

For a negated universal quantifier, if $\sim(\forall x)A$ is in the branch then $\sim A(x := a)$ is in the branch for some name a appearing in that branch. By hypothesis, $I(A(x := a)) = 0$ for this a, so $I((\forall x)A) = 0$ too, by the interpretation rule for the universal quantifier.

The cases for the existential quantifier and for its negation are no different to these, and I leave them for you to verify. The result shows that I satisfies *every* formula in the branch, and hence the formulas X at the top of the branch are all satisfied by I. In other words: if $X \not\vdash$ then $X \not\vDash$.

As a result, trees fit models hand-to-glove.

Now you have enough material to go away and analyse any predicate calculus argument form, using trees. There are no rules as to what order to do things in, but here are some hints to help make sure your proofs remain as small and manageable as they can be:

- Remember to always work on main connectives!
- Do the propositional rules first, if possible. *Especially if they do not branch.*
- Then do the particular instantiation rules.
- Do the general instantiation rules when it looks as if making a substitution will be interesting – for example, it will close off this branch, or will give you a model.
- Once you have a branch that looks as if it goes on forever, try to find a pattern in what goes into the branch, and summarise that in a table.
- Use that table to construct your model. Compress it into a smaller model if you prefer.

Howson's *Logic with Trees* [12] has good examples of trees for quantifiers. For much more of the theory of trees for predicate logic, you cannot go past Raymond Smullyan's *First-Order Logic* [29]: it is filled with insights and Smullyan has an unsurpassed depth of understanding of the tree method.

Exercises

Basic

{10.1} Test the following formulas, using trees. Are any tautologies? For those that are not, present counterexamples.

1 $(\exists x)Fx \equiv \sim(\forall x)\sim Fx$
2 $(\exists x)Fx \lor (\exists x)\sim Fx$
3 $(\forall x)(Fx \lor Gx) \supset ((\forall x)Fx \lor (\forall x)Gx)$
4 $(\exists x)(Fx \supset p) \supset ((\forall x)Fx \supset p)$
5 $(\forall x)Fx(Fx \supset Gx) \supset ((\forall x)Fx \supset (\forall x)Gx)$
6 $(\forall x)(Fx \lor Gx) \supset ((\forall x)Fx \lor (\exists x)Gx)$
7 $(\forall x)(Fx \,\&\, p) \supset ((\forall x)Fx \,\&\, p)$
8 $(\exists x)(Fx \supset (\forall y)Fy)$
9 $(\exists x)((\exists y)Fy \supset Fx)$
10 $(\exists x)(\forall y)(Fy \supset Fx)$

{10.2} Test these argument forms for validity, using trees. Present counterexamples to any invalid argument forms you find.

1 $(\forall x)((Fx \,\&\, Gx) \supset Hx) \vdash (\forall x)(Fx \supset (\sim Gx \lor Hx))$
2 $(\forall x)(\forall y)(Lxy \supset Mxy), (\forall x)(\forall y)(Lxy \supset Lyx) \vdash (\forall x)(\forall y)$
$(Mxy \supset Myx)$
3 $(\forall x)(\exists y)Lxy \vdash (\exists x)(\forall y)Lxy$
4 $(\forall x)(\forall y)(Lxy \supset Lyx), (\forall x)(\forall y)(\forall z)((Lxy \,\&\, Lyz) \supset Lxz) \vdash$
$(\forall x)((\exists y)Lxy \supset Lxx)$
5 $(\forall x)(\forall y)(Lxy \lor Lyx), (\forall x)(\forall y)(\forall z)((Lxy \,\&\, Lyz) \supset Lxz) \vdash$
$(\forall x)(\forall y)(\exists z)(Lxz \,\&\, Lyz)$

{10.3} Test all of the arguments formalised in Exercise 8.4.

{10.4} Construct an appropriate dictionary to formalise the following arguments, and test the resulting formalisations for validity:

1 PS is an axiomatic system. All of the theorems of PS are tautologies. No propositional variable is a tautology. All axiomatic systems of which no propositional variables are theorems are post-consistent. Therefore, PS is post-consistent.
2 If every decision is to be referred to the central authority then some programmes will be delayed. But all programmes have received approval, and nothing is to be delayed that has received approval. So, it follows that not every decision is to be referred to the central authority.

3   Whatever is true is not false and whatever is not false is true. If anything is false then no-one knows it. John knows something (and John is a person). So, something is true.

{10.5} A dyadic relation R is said to be *reflexive* iff $(\forall x)Rxx$, *symmetric* iff $(\forall x)(\forall y)(Rxy \supset Ryx)$ and *transitive* iff $(\forall x)(\forall y)(\forall z)((Rxy \,\&\, Ryz) \supset Rxz)$. Show that not all reflexive and symmetric relations are transitive by showing that

$$(\forall x)Rxx, (\forall x)(\forall y)(Rxy \supset Ryx) \nvdash$$
$$(\forall x)(\forall y)(\forall z)((Rxy \,\&\, Ryz) \supset Rxz)$$

Similarly, show that not all reflexive transitive relations are symmetric, and that not all symmetric transitive relations are reflexive.

{10.6} A dyadic relation R is said to have *no dead ends* iff $(\forall x)(\exists y)Rxy$. Show that all symmetric, transitive relations without dead ends are also reflexive by showing that

$$(\forall x)(\forall y)(Rxy \supset Ryx),$$
$$(\forall x)(\forall y)(\forall z)((Rxy \,\&\, Ryz) \supset Rxz,$$
$$(\forall x)(\exists y)Rxy \vdash (\forall x)Rxx$$

Advanced

{10.7} Consider the following two propositions:

$$(\forall x)(Mx \supset (\exists y)(Fy \,\&\, Oyx)) \quad (\forall x)(Fx \supset (\exists y)(My \,\&\, Ayx))$$

which you can read with the following dictionary:

$$Mx = x \text{ is male; } Fx = x \text{ is female;}$$

$$Oxy = x \text{ is the mother of } y; Axy = x \text{ is the father of } y$$

It should be clear that the two propositions are consistent and seem true. Every male person has a mother (who is female), and every female person has a father (who is male). Construct a model that satisfies these propositions, using a tree. In particular, explain what a completed tree for the two propositions looks like.

{10.8} Prove that in any closed tree, only a finite number of formulas have been resolved. This is *König's lemma*: any finite forking tree (any fork in the tree splits to a finite number of descendants) with finite branches is itself finite. This is in fact rather hard to prove. König proved it like this. Take a finite forking tree with infinitely many points in the tree. We show that it has an infinite branch as follows:

- Call a point in the tree *good* if it has an infinite number of descendants.
- The root of the tree is *good*.
- If a point in the tree is *good*, one of its children (immediate descendants) is *good*.
- Therefore there is an infinite branch in the tree.

Go through this proof and explain each step.

{10.9} Using the previous result, show that if $X \vdash A$ then there is a finite subset X^* of X where $X^* \vdash A$. This is the compactness theorem for predicate logic.

> The golden rule is that there
> are no golden rules.
> – George Bernard Shaw

Chapter 11

Identity and functions

The language of predicate logic is all well and good as it stands – it is a vast improvement over propositional logic – but there are still some things you cannot say. Say we have two names 'Clark Kent' and 'Superman', and we want to express the fact that they refer to the same person. We say it like this:

Clark Kent is Superman.

There is no way to say this simply in the language of first-order logic as we have it. The *is* in *Clark Kent is Superman* is not the same sort of *is* as appears in *Clark Kent is a reporter*. We cannot say *Sc* where *S* is the predicate *is Superman* and *c* is the name *Clark Kent*, for *Superman* is a name, just like *Clark Kent* is. There's nothing in the language that tells us that two names name the same thing. We must use a new predicate to ascribe the 'relation' that Clark Kent and Superman bear to each other in virtue of being the same person. (You can, of course, add a new two-place predicate *I* to the language for identity, and add premises to your arguments to govern the behaviour of I. But to do this would be to say that the argument 'Clark Kent is Superman, Clark Kent is over 2 metres tall, therefore Superman is over 2 metres tall' is invalid as it stands. It seems as if 'is' is not the sort of connective you must define every time you use it.)

Similarly, there is no way to say that two things are different. You can't say that there are two dogs in the room by saying

$$(\exists x)(Dx \ \& \ Rx) \ \& \ (\exists y)(Dy \ \& \ Ry)$$

since this will be true even if there's only one dog in the room. How can we extend our language to help us express such basic things as these?

Identity

We introduce a new predicate into our language to deal with such statements – it is a dyadic predicate written as '='. We write it 'infix' instead of 'prefix' because you are much more used to seeing '$a = b$' than seeing '$=ab$'. The formula

$$a = b$$

is true in a model just when a and b name the same object in that model, and it is false otherwise.

For the negation of $a = b$, we will not write '$\sim a = b$', which might be confusing. We will write $\sim(a = b)$, or, even better,

$$a \neq b$$

This is true in a model just when a and b name different objects in that model. Let's see how identity works in a particular model. Here is a model we have already seen:

$$D = \{d, k, e\}$$

$$I(a) = d$$
$$I(b) = k$$

	$I(P)$
d	1
k	1
e	0

$I(R)$	d	k	e
d	1	0	0
k	1	1	0
e	1	0	1

In this language, we can state more things than in the language without identity. For example, we can state that *Everyone reads someone else*. This is said by

$$(\forall x)(\exists y)(Rxy \ \& \ x \neq y)$$

This is false, since it is not true that for any person in the domain, there is someone else who they read. The instance

$$(\exists y)(Rdy \ \& \ d \neq y)$$

is false, since every instance

$$Rdd \ \& \ d \neq d \quad Rdk \ \& \ d \neq k \quad Rde \ \& \ d \neq e$$

is false. The first is false since $d \neq d$ is false; the second and third are false as Rdk and Rde are both false.

We can also state the claim: If you are read by everyone, you're Descartes. This is said by

$$(\forall x)((\forall y)Ryx \supset x = d)$$

This formula says: take anyone you like (this is x); then if everyone reads x, x must be identical to d. This is true in our model: the instances are:

$$(\forall y)Ryd \supset d = d \quad (\forall y)Ryk \supset k = d \quad (\forall y)Rye \supset e = d$$

The first instance is true because $d = d$ is true. For the second and the third to be true, $(\forall y)Ryk$ and $(\forall y)Rye$ must be false. These are both false because instances Rdk and Rde are false.

Now, to test arguments involving identity, we must have some tree rules featuring identity. The rules are of a similar form to others. We have a negated identity rule, and an identity rule. The *negated identity rule* is simple: Since all self-identities are true, a negated self-identity closes a branch:

A formula $a \neq a$ closes a branch in which it occurs.

The other rule we require – the *identity rule* – can be motivated like this: If $a = b$ is true, and we have something true of a, then that thing is also true of b, since a and b are the same thing. Let A be a formula in which a appears. $A(a := b)$ is a formula you get when you replace some instance of a in A by b. Our rule is then:

> If $a = b$ and A are in a branch, we can place $A(a := b)$ in that branch too.

Note that this does not resolve the formulas $a = b$ or A, for they can be used again.

We will use these rules to prove that $(\forall x)(\forall y)(x = y \supset y = x)$:

$$\sim(\forall x)(\forall y)(x = y \supset y = x) \checkmark a$$
$$|$$
$$\sim(\forall y)(a = y \supset y = a) \checkmark b$$
$$|$$
$$\sim(a = b \supset b = a)$$
$$|$$
$$a = b$$
$$b \neq a$$
$$b \neq b$$
$$\times$$

This tree applies the identity rules straightforwardly. We get $a = b$ and $b \neq a$. These do not immediately close the branch, since $b \neq a$ is the negation of $b = a$, and that is a different formula from $a = b$. (Proving that $b = a$ amounts to the same thing as $a = b$ is what we are trying to prove in this tree. It will do no good to just assume it!) So, we apply the identity rule to $a = b$ and $b = a$. Using $a = b$, we can replace the a in $b \neq a$ by a b. This then gives us $b \neq b$, which closes the branch, and hence the whole tree.

Trees with identity that close are very much like trees without identity that close. There is one extra wrinkle in dealing with trees with identity that do not close. We must ensure that the identity predicate on the domain is interpreted by the identity relation on that domain. This means that we may not always take the domain constructed from the model to just have one object per name, as the following example shows. Here is an example of a tree that does not close – we test $(\forall x)(\forall y)(\forall z)(((Rxy \ \& \ Rzx) \ \& \ y = z) \supset Rxx)$ below:

$$\sim(\forall x)(\forall y)(\forall z)(((Rxy \ \& \ Rzx) \ \& \ y = z) \supset Rxx) \ \checkmark a$$
$$|$$
$$\sim(\forall y)(\forall z)(((Ray \ \& \ Rza) \ \& \ y = z) \supset Raa) \ \checkmark b$$
$$|$$
$$\sim(\forall z)(((Rab \ \& \ Rza) \ \& \ b = z) \supset Raa) \ \checkmark c$$
$$|$$
$$\sim(((Rab \ \& \ Rca) \ \& \ b = c) \supset Raa) \ \checkmark$$
$$|$$
$$(Rab \ \& \ Rca) \ \& \ b = c \ \checkmark a$$
$$\sim Raa$$
$$|$$
$$Rab$$
$$Rca$$
$$b = c$$
$$|$$
$$Rac$$
$$\uparrow$$

And this branch is *open*. To deal with the open branch and to construct a countermodel, you must understand how to cope with identity. That's rather simple. In a model, identity is always denoted by the identity relation. In other words $I(=)$ relates two objects in the domain just when they're the same object. So, how do you construct a countermodel from an open branch? You do that by picking out names as domain elements, just as before, except for when some names denote the same object in the model. In that case, you just choose one of the constants to be a domain element, and it stands for all of the others too. Here, the open branch gives us three names: a, b, c. However, we know that $b = c$. So, the names form two *cliques*:

$$\{a\} \quad \{b,c\}$$

To construct the model, you take a *representative* from each clique to form the domain. Any property had by *one* member is had by all members. (This is no problem, since if $b = c$ and some property holds of b, it must hold of c too, by virtue of the identity rule for trees.) So, in our case, the facts known of the model go as follows:

$I(R)$	a	b
a	0	1
b	1	

We have Rba, since we have Rca, and $b = c$. We do not have Rbb (or its negation), as none of Rbb, Rcb, Rbc or Rcc appears in the branch. This is the information given by the branch, and it follows that either interpretation given to extend this by placing a 0 or a 1 in that space will do as an interpretation that makes the formula false. Therefore, it is not a tautology.

Translating some common quantifiers

In everyday language, we don't only use the quantifiers 'every' and 'some'. We also say things like 'at least 3', or 'at most 40' or 'exactly 3088'. We can express these using our own quantifiers along with equality. Here's how it goes.

At least n things are F is translated as

$$(\exists x_1) \cdots (\exists x_n)(Fx_1 \& \cdots \& Fx_n \& x_1 \neq x_2 \& x_1 \neq x_3 \& \cdots \& x_{n-1} \neq x_n)$$

In other words, there are n things that are F, where no pair taken from them is identical. For example, there are at least three logic students is translated as

$$(\exists x)(\exists y)(\exists z)(Lx \& Ly \& Lz \& x \neq y \& x \neq z \& y \neq z)$$

At most n things are F is translated as

$$(\forall x_1) \cdots (\forall x_{n+1})((Fx_1 \& \cdots \& Fx_{n+1}) \supset$$
$$(x_1 = x_2 \vee x_1 = x_3 \vee \cdots \vee x_n = x_{n+1}))$$

In other words, if we have '$n + 1$ things' that are F then we have at least double-counted: at least two of them are the same. For example, there are at most two logic students is translated as

$$(\forall x)(\forall y)(\forall z)((Lx \& Ly \& Lz) \supset (x = y \vee x = z \vee y = z))$$

You can put these two together to say that *exactly n things are F*. This can be translated as the conjunction of *at least n things are F* and *at most n things are F*.

A final case that is a little simpler than the general case for *exactly n* is the case for *exactly one* thing is F. This can be translated as follows:

$$(\exists x)(Fx \& (\forall y)(Fy \supset x = y))$$

In other words, it can be read as saying two things.

- There is something with property F.
- Anything with property F is identical to *that* thing.

If both are true then there must be exactly one thing with property F. If the first is false then there is not exactly one thing with property F, since there is nothing with property F. If the first is true but the second is false then there is not exactly one thing with property F, because there are more things with that property. So, our translation works.

As a final example, there is exactly one Indonesian logic student is translated as

$$(\exists x)(Ix \& Lx \& (\forall y)((Iy \& Lx) \supset x = y))$$

Exercise 11.8 asks you to use these definitions to show how basic facts about arithmetic can be derived from logic.

Functions

Sometimes – especially when you are modelling mathematical theories – predicates, names and identity are not sufficient to straightforwardly express all that we want to express. Suppose we are reasoning about numbers. We are able to add them and subtract them, multiply them and divide them. We have names for numbers, and addition, subtraction, multiplication and division are names for *functions*, which, when given numbers, return more numbers.

There is no straightforward way to represent functions in the language we have so far. It is technically possible to represent the addition function by the three-place predicate S where

$$Sxyz$$

means 'adding x to y gives you z'. Then you must state conditions that make S represent a genuine function: we have to state that for any x and y you like, there's exactly one z where $Sxyz$. We've already seen how to do this:

$$(\forall x)(\forall y)(\exists z)(Sxyz \;\&\; (\forall w)(Sxyw \supset z = w))$$

This says that, given any two inputs x and y, there is an output z, and any output from x and y must be equal to z. This is enough to make S represent a genuine function. However, dealing with a three-place predicate S is just too difficult. If we want to say that for any numbers x, y and z, $x + (y + z) = (x + y) + z$, we say

$$(\forall x)(\forall y)(\forall z)(\forall w)((\exists u)(Sxuw \;\&\; Syzu) \equiv (\exists v)(Sxyv \;\&\; Svzw))$$

which doesn't look a great deal like what we are trying to say.

An easier way to deal with this is to be explicit about functions, and to allow symbols that represent functions into our language. A function symbol is like a predicate, in that it has an arity, but it differs from a predicate, because a predicate applied to a number of names gives us a formula. A function symbol applied to a number of names gives us another name. For example, if f is a unary function symbol, and a and b are names, so are

$$fa \quad fb \quad ffa \quad fffb$$

Since a is a name, fa is a name. Since fa is a name, ffa is a name too. Similarly, if g is a two-place function symbol then

$$gab \quad gfab \quad gfaffb$$

are all names too. Sometimes, given repeated function applications, it helps to use parentheses to clarify how the order of expression works. Each of the names displayed above is

$$g(a,b) \quad g(f(a),b) \quad g(f(a),f(f(b)))$$

But these parentheses are, strictly speaking, irrelevant. Provided that the arity of each function symbol is known, there is exactly one way to understand each of the parentheses-free names.

So, sum and product are both two-place functions. We *often* give them special names, + and ×, and we *often* write them 'infix', between the names to which they apply, instead of before them. This is merely a notational convenience. Given these names, if a and b are names in our language, the following are also names:

$$a + b \quad a + (b \times c) \quad ((a \times a) \times b) + b \quad (a \times b) + (b \times a)$$

Function symbols are interpreted by functions on the domain. If f is a monadic function symbol and g a dyadic function symbol, and the domain $D = \{a, b, c\}$, then we can interpret function symbols in a little table:

	$I(f)$	$I(g)$	a	b	c
a	b	a	a	b	c
b	c	b	b	c	a
c	c	c	c	a	b

In this interpretation, we have $f(a) = b$, $f(b) = c$ and $f(c) = c$. The tables tell you the output value for every input value in the domain. Similarly, we have $g(a, a) = a$, $g(a, b) = b$, $g(b, c) = c$, and so on. The square table is read in row–column pairs to get the output of the function $I(g)$ from every input pair.

There is no need to modify any of our tree rules or to add any in order to use function symbols in trees.[1] Once function symbols are added to the language, the existing tree rules determine how they operate. Here is a tree testing $(\forall x)Lxf(x) \vdash (\forall x)(\exists y)Lxy$:

$$(\forall x)Lxf(x) \quad \backslash a$$
$$\sim(\forall x)(\exists y)Lxy \checkmark a$$
$$|$$
$$\sim (\exists y)Lay \quad \backslash f(a)$$
$$|$$
$$Laf(a)$$
$$|$$
$$\sim Laf(a)$$
$$\times$$

In this tree, we see some of the distinctives of using function symbols. If a is a name, and f a one-place function symbol, then $f(a)$ is a name too. We were able to substitute $f(a)$ in the general formula $\sim(\exists y)Lay$ in order to close the tree.

However, not only is $f(a)$ a name, so is $f(f(a))$, $f(f(f(a)))$, and so on, ad infinitum. As a result, any tree featuring function symbols *already* has an infinite number of names. If there are any general formulas to be used in a branch, that branch *must* be infinite if completed. There are very few *simple* open trees featuring function symbols. Here is one to show you how they look – this tree tests $(\forall x)Lxf(x) \vdash (\exists x)Lf(x)x$:

$$(\forall x)Lxf(x) \quad \backslash a, f(a), ff(a), \ldots$$
$$\sim(\exists y)Lf(x)x \checkmark a, f(a), ff(a), \ldots$$
$$|$$
$$Laf(a)$$
$$|$$
$$\sim Lf(a)a$$
$$|$$
$$Lf(a)ff(a)$$
$$|$$

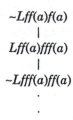

$$\sim Lff(a)f(a)$$
$$|$$
$$Lff(a)fff(a)$$
$$|$$
$$\sim Lfff(a)ff(a)$$
$$\cdot$$
$$\cdot$$
$$\cdot$$

The branch is open, and it continues forever. The objects named in the tree are a, $f(a)$, $ff(a)$, $fff(a)$,. . . . And the information in the tree is summarised by this table:

$I(L)$	a_1	a_2	a_3	a_4	...		$I(f)$
a_1		1				a_1	a_2
a_2	0		1			a_2	a_3
a_3		0		1		a_3	a_4
a_4			0			a_4	a_5

In this interpretation, we have an infinite domain $\{a_1, a_2, a_3,. . .\}$, and f is interpreted by a function that takes each domain element into the next one along in the list. Any interpretation that fills out the rest of the table will make the premise of the argument true and the conclusion false. One way to make the domain *smaller* is to use the trick we used in the last chapter: pay attention to what is explicitly said about what objects cannot be the same. Here we know that a_1 and a_3 are different, since a_1 is related by L to a_2, but a_3 is not related by L to a_2. Similarly, a_2 cannot be the same object as a_4, and a_3 differs from a_5, and so on. One way to arrange this is to identify every *third* object. We get this table:

$I(L)$	a_1	a_2	a_3		$I(f)$
a_1	0	1	0	a_1	a_2
a_2	0	0	1	a_2	a_3
a_3	1	0	0	a_3	a_1

There is a lot more that can be done with these extensions of our language. For more details, see the exercises.

Summary

- Identity is a special two-place relation, holding between x and y if and only if x and y are the same thing.
- We use the two-place relation '=' to represent identity.
- In a tree, a formula of the form $a \neq a$ closes a branch.
- In a tree, if a branch contains $a = b$ and a formula containing a, you can add to that branch the formula given by replacing any number of instances of a in that formula by b.
- We can use identity to represent numerical quantifiers such as *at least n, at most n* and *exactly n.*
- *Function symbols* represent functions, in our languages. Each function symbol is interpreted by a *function*. For example, a two-place function symbol is interpreted as a function from pairs of objects in the domain to objects in the domain.
- Function symbols use no new tree rules.

Exercises

Basic

{11.1} Use the dictionary

$$a = \text{Alphonzo}$$
$$b = \text{Bernadette}$$
$$c = \text{Candide}$$
$$Px = x \text{ is a person}$$
$$Rx = x \text{ is rich}$$
$$Sxy = x \text{ is smaller than } y$$
$$Wxy = x \text{ works for } y$$

to translate the following formulas:

1 $a = b$
2 $(a = b \ \& \ a \neq c)$

3   $(\exists x)((Px \ \& \ c \neq x) \ \& \ Rx)$

4   $(\forall x)((Px \ \& \ c \neq x) \supset Rx)$

5   $(\forall x)((Px \ \& \ b \neq x) \supset Sxb)$

6   $\sim(\exists x)((Px \ \& \ b \neq x) \ \& \ Sxc)$

7   $(\forall x)(Px \supset (\exists y)(Py \ \& \ Wxy))$

8   $(\forall x)(Px \supset (\exists y)(x \neq y \ \& \ (Py \ \& \ Wxy)))$

9   $(\exists x)(Px \ \& \ (\exists y)(Py \ \& \ Wxy))$

10 $(\exists x)(Px \ \& \ (\exists y)(x \neq y \ \& \ (Py \ \& \ Wxy)))$

{11.2} Using the same dictionary, formalise these expressions:

1   Alphonzo is rich but Candide is not.

2   Somebody who is rich is smaller than Candide.

3   Somebody other than Candide is smaller than Alphonzo.

4   Everyone is smaller than someone.

5   Everyone is smaller than someone other than themselves.

6   Everyone other than Alphonzo works for someone.

7   No-one (except Bernadette) works for Alphonzo.

8   There are at least two people.

9   There are at most three people.

10 There is exactly one person who works for Alphonzo.

{11.3} Test the following formulas. Find counterexamples to any that are not tautologies.

1   $(\forall x)x = x$

2   $(\forall x)(\forall y)(x = y \supset y = x)$

3   $(\forall x)(\exists y)x = y$

4   $(\forall x)(\forall y)(\forall z)((x = y \ \& \ y = z) \supset x = z)$

5   $(\forall x)(\forall y)(\forall z)(\forall w)((Rxy \ \& \ Rzw) \supset (y \neq z \vee Rxw))$

{11.4} Test the following arguments, and find counterexamples to those that are not valid:

1   $(\forall x)(Fx \supset Gx)$, $(\forall x)(Fx \supset x = a)$, therefore Ga

2   $(\forall x)(\forall y)x = y$, therefore $(\forall x)Gx \vee \sim(\forall x)Gx$

{11.5} Formalise and test these arguments:

1   At most two frogs are blue; therefore at most three frogs are blue.

2   At least two frogs are blue; therefore at least three frogs are blue.

{11.6} Show that $a = b \vdash f(a) = f(b)$. Does the converse hold? That is, does $f(a) = f(b) \vdash a = b$?

Advanced

{11.7} We have represented *exactly n things are F* as the conjunction of *at most n things are F* and *at least n things are F*. The resulting formula contains $2n+1$ quantifiers. Show that this is too wasteful by finding a more economical representation: one that uses only $n+1$ quantifiers.

{11.8} Show that basic arithmetic follows from the definitions of numerical quantifiers. That is, show that if *at least n things are F*, and *m things are G*, and *nothing is both F and G*, then *at least n + m things are either F or G*. Show that if *at most n things are F*, and *at most m things are G*, then *at most n + m things are either F or G*.

{11.9} How can you use numerical quantifiers to prove things about multiplication in the way we have used them for addition?

{11.10} You can formalise 'number theory' directly. The theory *Robinson's Arithmetic* has seven axioms, in the language with identity, the one-place function symbol s (the successor function), the name 0, and two two-place function symbols + (sum) and × (product), both written infix.

1    $(\forall x)(\forall y)(s(x) = s(y) \supset x = y)$

2    $(\forall x)0 \neq s(x)$

3    $(\forall x)(0 \neq x \supset (\exists y)s(y) = x)$

4    $(\forall x)(x + 0 = x)$

5    $(\forall x)(x + s(y) = s(x + y))$

6    $(\forall x)(x \times 0 = 0)$

7    $(\forall x)(x \times s(y) = (x \times y) + x))$

The first three axioms say respectively: no two numbers have the same successor; zero is not a successor; and every number other than zero is a successor. The next two axioms dictate the behaviour of sum, and the last two the behaviour of product. Call the set of the seven axioms RA.

In this language, we can use 1 as a shorthand for $s(0)$, 2 as a shorthand for $s(s(0))$, and so on. Prove the following results:

1 $RA \vdash 2 + 2 = 4.$
2 $RA \vdash 2 + 2 \neq 5$
3 $RA \vdash 2 \times 3 = 6$
4 $RA \vdash 2 \times 3 \neq 5$
5 $RA < (\forall x)(\forall y)(x + y = y + x)$

(The last question is *remarkably* more difficult than the first four. For this, you must construct a model of all of RA that doesn't $(\forall x)(\forall y)(x + y = y + x)$ true too.)

> All animals are equal
> but some animals are more equal than others.
> – George Orwell

Note

1 You must remember, however, that with the positive existential and negative universal rules, you introduce new *names*, not new function *symbols*. If you learn that $(\exists x)Gx$ then you are entitled to say Ga (where a is a *new* name) – you are of course not entitled to deduce $Gf(a)$, for that would be to assume something about the object with property G, namely that it is also the result of applying the function f to some object. That might not be the case.

Chapter 12

Definite descriptions

Names in our languages pick out objects. In our formal language, this job is done by names, which are completely *atomic* (they have no significant parts) or are given by applying *function symbols* to other names. There is no other class of referring expressions in our language.

This seems like an odd fit. We have shown how for formulas, the meanings (interpretations) of complex formulas are made up out of the meanings of simpler formulas. It seems that things should work like this for referring expressions too. There seem to be *descriptions* that pick out objects, in virtue of the predicates in those descriptions. Descriptions such as the tallest person in the room or the cause of that disease seem to *act like* referring expressions, and it seems that the structure and meaning of the description determines the referent, which is picked out by that description. This fact is not recognised by the language we have so far. There is no way to get a name that depends in any way on a predicate.

Furthermore, descriptions seem to feature in some paradoxes, or strange phenomena, which ought to be clarified. Here are just two ways that descriptions seem odd when compared with other names or terms in our language.

Failures of bivalence

Descriptions seem to mandate failures of bivalence. For example, *the present king of France is bald* is not true, as France does not have a king at present. Similarly, the present king of France is not bald is not true, for the same reason. This is unlike other names, for which one of *a is bald* and *a is not bald* are true (except, perhaps, for reasons of the vagueness of the term bald. Please ignore that for the moment, or, if you can't, please pick a precise predicate). It would be good to have some explanation of why descriptions allow such things.

Non-existence claims

Along similar lines, descriptions enable us to claim that certain things do not exist. It makes perfect sense to say there is no present king of France, and furthermore, it is true. We can't do this with *names* in our language. Every name denotes an object in the domain, and so each name refers to an object that exists (at least in the sense of the *existential quantifier*).

What can we do about descriptions? Can we clarify these issues?

Russell's solution

Bertrand Russell came up with a nice solution to these puzzles, by giving an analysis of descriptions in terms of the language we already have at hand. His solution was given in 1905 [24] and it is an enduring testimony to the way that formal logic can be used to enlighten some rather difficult issues.

Recall that we can translate *exactly one thing is F* as

$$(\exists x)(Fx \ \& \ (\forall y)(Fy \supset x = y))$$

A *definite description* is a term in the language such as '*the F*'. Russell analysed definite descriptions using our translation of *exactly one thing is F*

In normal discourse, when there is exactly one thing with property *F*, it is common to describe the object in question as 'the *F*' – for example, we talk about

The Prime Minister of Australia
The person who last climbed Mt Everest
The thing I'm trying to remember

and many other things like that. Russell noticed that when we do talk in this way, we are presupposing a number of things. We are presupposing that there is something that satisfies the description (there *is* a Prime Minister of Australia) and we are presupposing that there is at most one of them (there is *no more than one* Prime Minister of Australia). If the first condition were not met then any talk of *the* F would be mistaken, as there would be nothing fitting the bill. If the second condition were not met, the talk would still be mistaken: we should talk about *an* F, not *the* F. So, Russell went ahead and used these facts to give an *analysis* of definite descriptions.

Russell's analysis goes like this: whenever I say that *the F is a G*, I am stating that

- There *is* an *F*.
- There is *no more than one F*.
- That thing with property *F* also has property *G*.

So, to say *the F is a G* formally, I am stating the following:

$$(\exists x)(Fx \mathbin{\&} (\forall y)(Fy \supset y = x) \mathbin{\&} Gx)$$

Something has property *F*, nothing else has that property, and this thing has property *G* too. We will introduce a bit of notation as a shorthand. We write that formula for *the F is a G* in shorthand as

$$(Ix)(Fx, Gx)$$

We can use this to translate claims involving definite descriptions. For example, the claim *The Prime Minister is in the Liberal Party, and is short* becomes

$$(Ix)(Px, Lx \ \& \ Sx)$$

where P, L and S stand for the obvious properties. Of course, we could have translated this as

$$(Ix)(Px, Lx) \ \& \ (Ix)(Px, Sx)$$

which comes to the same thing.

The Prime Minister is shorter than the Deputy Prime Minister is more complex to translate. A halfway translation is

$$(Ix)(Px, x \text{ is shorter than the deputy P. M.})$$

Now, if Sxy is *x is shorter than y*, and Dx is *x is a Deputy P. M.*, then how can we say *x is shorter than the deputy P. M.*? We say *the deputy P. M. is F* by saying $(Iy)(Dy, Fy)$ (y is a better variable to choose than x, now that x is in use). What is the property F had by the deputy P. M.? The property we want is x being shorter than him. So, the property we need for Fy is Sxy. We get, in full,

$$(Ix)(Px, (Iy)(Dy, Sxy))$$

Complex translations involving definite descriptions are not always easy. You should ask, given an object described by a definite description: How is it described? This goes in the first slot. And: What property does it have? This goes in the second slot.

We can create tree rules for (Ix) by writing out the tree rules for its definition. The (Ix) rule is

$$(Ix)(Fx, Gx)$$
$$|$$
$$Fa \qquad (a \text{ is new})$$
$$(\forall y)(Fy \supset y = a)$$
$$Ga$$

And the negated (Ix) rule is

$$\sim(Ix)(Fx, Gx)$$

$$\sim Fa \quad (\forall y)(Fy \supset y = a) \quad \sim Ga$$

And this rule can be applied for *any* name a. We can use these rules to test the argument form 'if the F is G, then there is an F':

$$(Ix)(Fx, Gx) \checkmark a$$
$$\sim(\exists x)Fx \quad \backslash a$$
$$|$$
$$Fa$$
$$(\forall y)(Fy \supset y = a)$$
$$Ga$$
$$|$$
$$\sim Fa$$
$$\times$$

The next tree is more complex – it shows that from $(Ix)(Fx, Gx)$ you can deduce $(\forall x)(\forall y)((Fx \ \& \ Fy) \supset x = y)$:

$$(Ix)(Fx, Gx) \checkmark a$$
$$\sim(\forall x)(\forall y)((Fx \ \& \ Fy) \supset x = y) \checkmark b$$
$$|$$
$$Fa$$
$$(\forall y)(Fy \supset y = a) \quad \backslash b, c$$
$$Ga$$
$$|$$
$$\sim(\forall y)((Fb \ \& \ Fy) \supset b = y) \checkmark b$$
$$|$$
$$\sim((Fb \ \& \ Fc) \supset b = c)$$
$$|$$
$$Fb \ \& \ Fc$$
$$b \neq c$$
$$|$$
$$Fb$$
$$Fc$$
$$|$$

(continued on next page)

$$Fb \supset b = a$$

$$\overset{\diagup \qquad \diagdown}{\underset{\times}{\sim Fb} \qquad b = a}$$

$$|$$

$$Fc \supset c = a$$

$$\overset{\diagup \qquad \diagdown}{\underset{\times}{\sim Fc} \qquad c = a}$$

$$|$$

$$a \neq c$$

$$|$$

$$a \neq a$$

$$\times$$

Russell's analysis of definite descriptions has given us a way to analyse terms that use predicates in their construction. The analysis tells us how these terms are related to other parts of our language. The analysis also gives us specific answers to the two problems noted earlier:

Failures of bivalence

For example, *the present king of France is bald* is not true, as France does not have a king at present. This is explained because $(Ix)(Kx,Bx)$ fails, since there is nothing with property K. Similarly, *the present king of France is not bald* is not true, as $(Ix)(Kx,\sim Bx)$ fails, as there is nothing with property K. However, this is not a real failure of the law of the excluded middle, as the negation of $(Ix)(Kx,Bx)$ is not $(Ix)(Kx,\sim Bx)$, but $\sim(Ix)(Kx,Bx)$. This formula is true.

Nonexistence claims

'There is no present king of France' is not saying of an object that it does not exist. It is saying that there is nothing with the property of being a present king of France: $\sim(\exists x)Fx$. This is not a problem.

Definite descriptions, for Russell, are not referring expressions in the way that names are. They are descriptions, which are implicit existential quantifications. The puzzles about failures of excluded middles and non-existence claims fade away when they are properly understood. The apparatus of formal logic has helped clarify the structure of this part of our language.

Nuances

Russell's analysis of definite descriptions is certainly clarifying, but like all simple philosophical analyses, it is limited. The analysis gets some uses of definite descriptions right, but others it gets wrong.

Limited domains

First, the analysis says nothing about restrictions on the domain. I might say *the top logic student will win a prize*. I don't mean *the top logic student* but *the top logic student in my class this year*. Typically, our descriptions don't pin down one thing, unless we restrict the domain of quantification in some way. Russell's account gives us no insight into how that is done.

Referential uses

Second, sometimes people use definite descriptions to describe things, and succeed, even though the predicates used don't describe the object referred to. For example, at a party, I might talk about the man in the corner drinking the martini, and you nod, and we talk about him. We succeed in referring to him, even if he's not drinking a martini! If it happened to be a glass of water, my description failed to describe him correctly, but the mere fact that you and I both thought it was a martini was enough to 'fix the referent'. Russell's account gives us no insight into how this works, and in fact, it seems to get this account completely wrong. According to Russell, all of my claims involving 'the man in the corner drinking the martini' are false if there is no such man, or, worse, are referring to someone else, if there happens to be another man in the corner who (unbeknownst to us) is actually drinking a martini. More must be said about definite descriptions to explain how this phenomenon works.

Further reading

Russell's original paper [24] is still excellent reading. An extended discussion of Russell's analysis is found in Miller's *Philosophy of Language* [19].

Chapter 8 of Bostock's *Intermediate Logic* [2] and Chapter 4 of Grayling's *Introduction to Philosophical Logic* [8] also contain good discussions of definite descriptions.

Exercises

{12.1} With the dictionary

$$a = \text{Alphonzo}$$
$$b = \text{Bernadette}$$
$$c = \text{Candide}$$
$$Vx = x \text{ is a Vice-Chancellor}$$
$$Lx = x \text{ is a Lord Mayor}$$
$$Fx = x \text{ is flies}$$
$$Hx = x \text{ is a horse}$$
$$Sxy = x \text{ is swifter than } y$$

translate the following, using the I shorthand for definite descriptions:

1   The Vice-Chancellor flies.
2   The Lord-Mayor is a horse.
3   The flying horse is swifter than Bernadette.
4   Alphonzo is a Lord Mayor.
5   Alphonzo is the Lord Mayor.
6   Candide is swifter than the non-flying horse.
7   The flying horse is swifter than the horse that does not fly.
8   The flying horse is swifter than a horse that does not fly.

9 Everything other than the flying horse is swifter than the flying horse.

10 Alphonzo is swifter than the Vice-Chancellor, but Bernadette is swifter than the flying horse.

{12.2} Translate away the definite description connectives in your answers to the previous question, using Russell's analysis of definite descriptions.

{12.3} Test the following argument forms for validity, presenting any counterexample you find.

1 $(Ix)(Fx, Gx)$ & $(Ix)(Fx, Hx)$ therefore $(Ix)(Fx, Gx$ & $Hx)$

2 $(Ix)(Fx$ & $Gx, Hx)$ therefore $(Ix)(Fx, Hx)$

3 $(Ix)(Fx, Gx)$ therefore $(\forall x)(\sim Gx \supset \sim Fx)$

4 $(Ix)(Fx, \sim Gx)$ therefore $\sim(Ix)(Fx, Gx)$

5 $Fa, (Ix)(Fx, Gx)$ therefore $(Ix)(Fx, x = a)$

{12.4} What does it mean to say $(Ix)(Fx, Fx)$?

When in the chronicle of wasted time
I see descriptions of the fairest wights.
– William Shakespeare

Chapter 13

Some things do not exist

Existential import and predicates

According to the syllogistic logic of Aristotle, the following arguments are valid:

> All tigers are dangerous.
> So some tigers are dangerous.
>
> No liars are honest.
> So some liars are not honest.

Aristotle's syllogistic logic dominated logical theory in Western civilisation for over 2,000 years. According to the predicate logic we have considered, both arguments have the *invalid* forms

$$(\forall x)(Fx \supset Gx) \text{ therefore } (\exists x)(Fx \ \& \ Gx)$$
$$\sim(\exists x)(Fx \ \& \ Gx) \text{ therefore } (\exists x)(Fx \ \& \sim Gx)$$

The reason for the difference is straightforward. For syllogistic logic, an assumption was made that every category is inhabited. That is, every predicate has something in its extension. If all tigers are dangerous, pick one of the tigers. It is dangerous. Therefore some tiger is dangerous. Similarly, if no liars are honest, pick one of the liars. He or she is dishonest. If there is no such tiger, or no such liar, the premises are true and the conclusion false.

Now you might ask how we could have learned the predicates 'liar' or 'tiger' if there weren't any of the required creatures to describe. So, you might think that the assumption that all our categories are inhabited is a good one. There seem to be other cases where this assumption fails. Assume that Newton's physics is correct. Then the premise of this argument is true, but the conclusion is false:

Any bodies unaffected by external forces move uniformly.
So some body unaffected by external forces moves uniformly.

The premise is given by Newton's laws of motion. Anything unaffected by external forces moves in one direction with constant velocity. The conclusion is false since every object exerts a (possibly very small) gravitational force on every other object. The property 'a body unaffected by external forces' is empty. The argument is invalid.

This diagnosis – that invalidity can come about by uninhabited predicates – is the one given by predicate logic. Any counter-example to either predicate argument form will be one in which F is interpreted as an empty property.

We say that Aristotle's syllogistic logic carries existential import because each of its categories or predicates is assumed to be inhabited. Predicate logic has no existential import for predicates because the formula

$$(\exists x)Fx$$

is not a tautology. The fact that we have a predicate F does not mean that the predicate is inhabited.

Existential import and names

Predicate logic is not without some existential import. Predicate logic has existential import for names. The formula

$$(\exists x)(x = a)$$

is a tautology, for any name a. This means that names are assumed to refer to existing objects. We allow empty predicates, but we do not allow empty names. This may or may not be a problem. One way in which it might be a problem seems to be the fact that many of us think that one of the following two sentences is true, and the other false:

There is something that is identical to John Howard.
There is something that is identical to Santa Claus.

The first of these is true and the second false. Assuming that John Howard and Santa Claus are both names, both of these sentences have the form $(\exists x)(x = a)$. So, we have some choices to make:

- Santa Claus exists.
- *Santa Claus* is not a name, and so *There is something that is identical to Santa Claus* does not have the form $(\exists x)(x = a)$.
- $(\exists x)(x = a)$ is not a tautology.

The first of these options *might* be appealing in the case of Santa Claus. However, it is hard to maintain that for every name there is something that exists that bears that name. At least some of Pegasus, Sherlock Holmes, Bilbo Baggins, Mickey Mouse and Superman do not exist. So, we can safely leave that option behind.

The second option holds that things that look like names, but that do not refer to objects, are not really names at all. We have already seen this sort of analysis in the previous chapter. Russell took it that a description such as the Prime Minister of Australia is not really a referring expression like a name, but really an existential quantification, which picks out an object by way of the predicates involved in the description. 'The Prime Minister of Australia is short' is a grammatically well-formed statement, even if Australia is going without a prime minister at the moment. There is no requirement that all our descriptions pick out objects.

Russell's analysis can be extended to deal not only with expressions that are explicitly descriptions. It can be used to apply to names too. The description theory of names holds that every name is really a hidden description. For example, when I use John Howard I might mean

That person named 'John Howard' by his parents, who appears in the news a lot at the moment.

No doubt, a more sophisticated account of what description is in play could be given. The important thing to see is how this goes when dealing with names (like Santa Claus) that do not pick out existing objects. The name Santa Claus can be paired with this description:

That fat man who often wears red with white fur who lives at the North Pole and gives presents at Christmas to everyone.

There is no doubt that some description like this is closely tied to the name Santa Claus. However, if we go on to analyse the definite description in the way Russell did, the following two sentences are both false:

Santa Claus lives in the North Pole.
Santa Claus lives in Nashville, with Elvis.

They are both false because there is no such person fitting the Santa Claus description. However, there is a sense in which these two claims are different. At least, according to the standard mythology about Santa Claus, the first is true and second is false. Perhaps there is a way of maintaining the difference between the two claims, by reading them as shorthand for the following two claims:

According to mythology, Santa Claus lives in the North Pole.
According to mythology, Santa Claus lives in Nashville, with Elvis.

The first is certainly true and the second is certainly false. This strategy (which we might call the *hidden prefix* strategy) does well in these cases, and in many others.

> According to Greek mythology, Pegasus is a flying horse.
> According to the Conan Doyle stories, Sherlock Holmes lived in Baker Street.

> According to Greek mythology, Pegasus has seventy-two heads.
> According to the Conan Doyle stories, Sherlock Holmes was a jazz singer.

The third and fourth of these claims are false. What is true of these fictional characters seems to be what the stories say about them – and what you can deduce from what is in the stories.

For all that success, some have found problems with the hidden prefix strategy. Many want to say that sentences that mix up fictions might still be true:

> Pegasus could fly higher than Sherlock Holmes.
> John Howard is shorter than Hercules.

The first claim here mixes up two different fictions. There is no mythology or story including both Pegasus and Sherlock Holmes. So why are some people tempted to say that this is true? Similarly, the second claim mixes up mythology and reality. Hercules was tall (but non-existent). John Howard is not tall. He is shorter than Hercules. However, that claim 'crosses the boundaries' between fiction and reality.

Some have thought that these problems, with both the description theory and the hidden prefix accounts, are so bad that we should look for another strategy. We must find an account of logic that allows names that do not denote.

Now one way to do this, without introducing a grammatical difference in the way we treat proper names, is what has been called free logic. The logic is *free of existential import*. A name doesn't have to pick out an existing object in order to function as a name. The language is the same as with standard predicate logic, except for the introduction of a new one-place predicate: $E!$. $E!a$ is true when a exists. Or, more formally, $E!a$ is true when the name a denotes an (existing) object. So, if a stands for Pegasus and b stands for John Howard then presumably $E!a$ is false, but $E!b$ is true.

Models

The version of free logic we will use has a domain, and predicates (and function symbols and identity, if you like) just like standard predicate logic. The predicate $E!$ is treated just like any other predicate. It divides the existent objects from the non-existent objects. Here is an example model:

	$I(H)$	$I(F)$	$I(E!)$	$I(S)$	a	b	c	d
a	1	1	0	a	0	0	0	0
b	1	0	1	b	1	0	0	0
c	0	0	1	c	1	1	0	1
d	0	1	0	d	1	1	0	0

In this model, H is shorthand for *is a horse*, F for *flies* and S for *is shorter than*. The objects a, b, c and d are respectively *Pegasus*, *Phar Lap* (a famous Australian racehorse), *John Howard* and *Superman*. This should explain the distribution of truth values in the tables. Ha and Hb are true, as Pegasus and Phar Lap are horses, Fa and Fd are true, because both Pegasus and Superman fly. The S table ensures that John Howard is shorter than Superman, who is shorter than Phar Lap, who is shorter than Pegasus. The only new thing is the interpretation of $E!$. Pegasus and Superman don't exist. Therefore, $E!a$ and $E!d$ fail.

This means that we ought to modify the interpretation of the existential quantifier to match this. We do not want to say that there exists a flying horse. $(\exists x)(Fx \,\&\, Hx)$ fails, so we must say that $Fa \,\&\, Ha$ is not an appropriate instance of $(\exists x)(Fx \,\&\, Hx)$. The appropriate instances of an existential quantifier are substitutions of names where we know that the names denote.

It follows that $(\exists x)(Fx \,\&\, Hx)$ is false, as is $(\exists x)(Fx \,\&\, {\sim}Hx)$. In this model, there is no flying *non*-horse either. In fact, in this model,

($\exists x$)Fx is false, as no appropriate instances (here the only appropriate instances are Fb and Fc) are true. Phar Lap might gallop very fast, but he does not fly.

This interpretation of the existential quantifier ($\exists x$) fixes the interpretation of the universal quantifier too, if we take ($\forall x$)A to be equivalent to ~($\exists x$)~A. Everything is A just when nothing is not A. ($\forall x$)A is true just when every appropriate instance of A is true. So, ($\forall x$)($Hx \supset$ ~Fx) is true in this model, since all (existing) horses do not fly.

Some have thought that it might be good to have more liberal quantifiers that range over all objects in the domain, instead of just the existing ones. We will look at how you might do this after we give tree rules for the system of free logic as we have defined it.

Tree rules

The rules for all of the connectives remain as they were. The rules for the quantifiers are modified slightly, to deal with the existence predicate:

Existential

To resolve a formula of the form ($\exists x$)A, extend any open branch in which the formula occurs with an instance of A using a new name that has not occurred in the branch before, and also add that this name denotes an object:

$$($\exists x$)A$$
$$|$$
$$E!a$$
$$A(x := a) \quad (a \text{ new})$$

Negated existential

Given a formula of the form ~($\exists x$)A, and a name a, you can extend any open branch in which the formula occurs by two branches – one containing ~$E!a$ and the other containing ~$A(x := a)$:

$$\sim(\exists x)A$$

$$\sim E!a \qquad \sim A(x := a) \text{ (any } a)$$

The universal rule works on the same principle.

Universal

Given a formula of the form $(\forall x)A$, and a name a, you can extend any open branch in which the formula occurs by any two branches – one containing $\sim E!a$, and the other containing $A(x := a)$:

$$\sim(\exists x)A$$

$$\sim E!a \qquad A(x := a) \text{ (any } a)$$

The negated universal rule is just like the existential rule:

Negated universal

To resolve a formula of the form $\sim(\forall x)A$, extend any open branch in which the formula occurs with $\sim A(x := a)$ and $E!a$, using a new name a:

$$(\exists x)A$$
$$|$$
$$E!a$$
$$\sim A(x := a) \quad (a \text{ new})$$

So, $(\exists x)A$ means that there exists some object a such that $A(x := a)$, and $(\forall x)A$ means that for any name a you like, $A(x := a)$ is true, or there is no object a. This seems to make sense, given our talk of Pegasus. We can treat these as proper names, and still agree that all horses don't fly, and that Pegasus is a flying horse. It's just that Pegasus is a non-existent flying horse. To check that this works out, we'll test the argument from $(\forall x)(Hx \supset \sim Fx)$ and Ha to $\sim Fa$:

$$(\forall x)(Hx \supset {\sim}Fx) \quad \backslash a$$
$$Ha$$
$$\sim\sim Fa$$

```
          ~~Fa
        ╱       ╲
    ~E!a      Ha ⊃ ~Fa
     ↑         ╱     ╲
            ~Ha      ~Fa
             ×        ×
```

The tree stays open. We have a model making the premise true and the conclusion false:

	$I(H)$	$I(F)$	$I(E!)$
a	1	1	0

In this model Ha is true, and $\sim Fa$ is clearly false. More interesting is the issue of whether $(\forall x)(Hx \supset {\sim}Fx)$ is true. It is – because *all of its appropriate instances are true*, or, more clearly, because *none of its appropriate instances are false*, since it has no instance here. In the domain, the only object we have is a, and it does not exist. Therefore, we have no instances to make our universally quantified premise false, and, as a result, it is true.

We will end this section with one more example. Box 13.1 shows a tree to test the argument with premises $(\forall x)(Fx \supset Gx)$ and $(\forall x)(Gx \supset Hx)$ and conclusion $(\forall x)(Fx \supset Hx)$. As one would hope, the tree closes, and the argument form is valid.

Nuances

The system of free logic discussed here has many desirable properties. However, there is more to be done to make it a satisfactory theoretical device. Here are some of the issues that we ought to address, and which point to further modifications of the theory.

Box 13.1

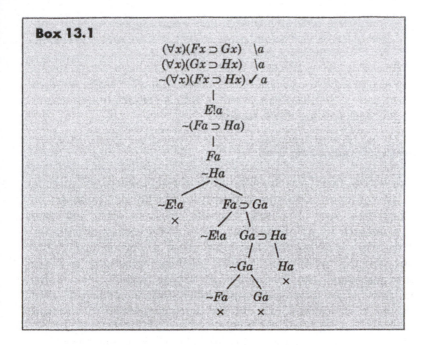

Bivalence

According to this account of free logic and non-existence, either
Sherlock Holmes had blood type AB or he did not have this type.
As far as I can tell, the Conan Doyle stories do not actually tell
us Holmes' blood type. There does not seem to be any reason for
preferring one type over another, yet the interpretation of free
logic assumes that, for every predicate, either it or its negation
applies to each object – including the non-existent ones. Exercise
13.3 asks you to look at a modification of the tree rules that allows
you to reject $Fa \lor \sim Fa$ when a does not denote.

Definite descriptions

Definite descriptions seem to apply in the case of non-existent
objects too. For example, the following claim seems to be true:

> Santa Claus is the fat man who often wears red with white fur who lives at the North Pole and gives presents at Christmas to everyone.

If I read it using Russell's analysis of definite descriptions, it comes out as false, as there is no fat man who *often* wears red with white fur. . . . So Russell's account of definite descriptions does not fit well with free logic as it stands.

Inner and outer quantification

One way to deal with this is to expand the language yet further, to allow for two sorts of quantification. The fat man living at the North Pole, who gives away presents, does not exist, but there is a fat man living at the North Pole who gives away presents. This may sound strange, but if we allow a new quantifier into our language (Sx), where $(Sx)Fx$ (read as 'something is F') is true just when some instance of Fx is true (whether or not this instance is an appropriate one) then $(Sx)Fx$ can be true, even though $(\exists x)Fx$ fails. Similarly, we can have $(Ax)Fx$ to be interpreted as saying that *every* instance of Fx is true. Then $(Sx)(Fx \ \& \ Hx)$ is true, as some horse flies (namely, Pegasus) and $(Ax)(Hx \supset \sim Fx)$ fails, as not all horses do not fly. This two-sorted kind of quantification is called inner and outer quantifiers. The inner quantifiers are the original $(\forall x)$ and $(\exists x)$, as these range over the inner domain of existing things. The new quantifiers (Ax) and (Sx) range over the outer domain of all things, existent and non-existent.

The intended interpretation

Once we start down this track, however, we face real difficulties in understanding our own models. What are these things that appear in the outer domain in the semantics? Are they concepts? If so, which concepts? Are they non-existent objects? If so, how do we tell how many of them there are? When we talk about existence, there is some kind of theoretical constraint that can be applied – such as Ockham's razor, and other theoretical constraints that help us decide when to say that something exists. It is very hard to see what can be said about demarcating the *outer domain*.

Further reading

Chapter 5 of Read's *Thinking about Logic* [21], Chapter 8 of Bostock's *Intermediate Logic* [2] and Chapter 4 of Grayling's *An Introduction to Philosophical Logic* [8] all have useful things to say about free logic. Richard Routley's article 'Some things do not exist' [23] is a defence of the quantification over non-existent objects, or *outer* quantification.

Exercises

Basic

{13.1} Using the rules of free logic, test these arguments:

1 $(\exists x)Fx$ therefore $(\exists x)(E!x \,\&\, Fx)$
2 $(\forall x)Fx$ therefore $(\exists x)Fx$
3 $(\forall x)(Gx \supset E!x)$, $E!a$ therefore $\sim Fa$

{13.2} Show that once we have a language containing *outer quantification* and $E!$, the inner quantifiers are also definable. That is, show that $(Ax)(E!x \supset Fx)$ is equivalent to $(\forall x)Fx$ and $(Sx)(E!x \,\&\, Fx)$ is equivalent to $(\exists x)Fx$.

Advanced

{13.3} To cope with the problem of the previous exercise, modify the rules of free logic so that $Fa_1\ldots a_n$ closes with $\sim Fa_1\ldots a_n$ only when a_1 to a_n all exist. What does the resulting logic look like? Is the result any better or worse than standard free logic?

{13.4} Prove the tree rules sound and complete for the models of free logic.

{13.5} Show that if an argument (without $E!$) is valid in free logic then it is valid in traditional predicate logic too. (There are two ways of doing this. You could use the fact that any model of traditional predicate logic is also a model of free logic. Or you could show that if a tree closes using the rules of free logic then the corresponding tree using the rules of traditional predicate logic also closes.)

{13.6} Show that free logic can be interpreted inside traditional predicate logic in the following way. For each formula, A define A^t like this. Select a new predicate E, then define inductively

$$(Fa_1 \ldots a_n)^t = Fa_1 \ldots a_n$$
$$(A \ \& \ B)^t = A^t \ \& \ B^t$$
$$(A \lor B)^t = A^t \lor B^t$$
$$(A \supset B)^t = A^t \supset B^t$$
$$(A \equiv B)^t = A^t \equiv B^t$$
$$(\sim A)^t = \sim A^t$$
$$((\exists x)A)^t = (\exists x)(Ex \ \& \ A^t)$$
$$((\forall x)A)^t = (\forall x)(Ex \supset A^t)$$

So the translation keeps everything the same, except for modifying the quantifiers. (This is called restricting the quantifiers by E – instead of saying that *something* is A, we say that some E is A; instead of saying that everything is A, we say that every E is A.)

Show that $X^t \vdash A^t$ in classical logic if and only if $X \vdash A$ is valid in free logic.

{13.7} Construct tree rules for outer quantification, and show that they too are sound and complete for the interpretation of free logic with outer quantifiers.

> The brilliant Cerebus
> discovered three different kinds of dragon:
> the mythical, the chimerical
> and the purely hypothetical.
> They were all, one might say, non-existent,
> but each non-existed in an entirely different way.
> – Stanislaw Lem

Chapter 14

What is a predicate?

We will introduce the topic of this chapter by considering an argument.

An argument

Here is an argument, due to René Descartes, designed to show that reality is not merely material – there are some immaterial things too.

> I can now imagine that my material body is not now existing.
> I can not now imagine that I am not now existing.
> Therefore, I am not now my material body.

This is an argument for *dualism*, the view that the universe contains immaterial things (souls, minds, gods, and things like that) as well as material things (bodies, tables, chairs, trees, and so on). Read the argument closely. Do you think it is valid? Do you think it is sound? Try formalising the argument. Is the form valid?

What can we say about Descartes' argument? Before examining the form of the argument, let's look at the premises.

Premise 1

Here is how Descartes can reason to justify the first premise. Knowledge of material things comes through the senses. I can imagine that I am tricked by an evil demon with great powers, who gives me false sensations. Everything I hear, see, smell, feel, taste and touch might be the result of this trickery! The appearances might not correspond to any external reality at all. So, I can imagine my material body not now existing.

Premise 2

Descartes could reason like this to justify the second premise. In order for me to imagine that *I* do not exist, I have to think about the issue. *I* have to do the imagining. But if I am thinking about the issue, I must exist in order to be doing the thinking. So, I cannot now imagine that I am not now thinking. (This is the famous *cogito ergo sum*: 'I think, therefore I am'.)

These two lines of reasoning are used by Descartes to justify the premises. They are very interesting in their own right, but we will not pause to examine these any further. To be sure of the soundness of the argument, you must examine the premises, but you also need to examine the validity of the argument, and it is to this that we now turn.

To check the validity, we can formalise the argument, and then test it using trees or whatever other technique we have at hand. Its form seems simple:

$$Fa, \sim Fb \text{ therefore } a = b$$

where a names my body, b names *me* and 'Fx' is 'I can now imagine x not existing'. This form is certainly valid. Its validity comes from the rule for identity. If $a = b$ and Fa, I can deduce Fb.

Understanding the argument

However, things are not *that* simple. It is important to understand whether or not our translation is adequate to the task of explaining the validity of this argument. There seems to be good reason to believe, in this case, that it doesn't. A common objection made to the Dualist argument, an objection made by Gottfried Leibniz, goes like this. The argument doesn't *really* have this translation, since what I can imagine about a thing isn't a property of that thing. It is rather a property of me and of my cognitive capacity. If we want to use 'property' in this wide sense, to allow my thoughts about objects to be properties of those objects, then we have problems with our rules for identity. For instance, consider this argument:

> I can now imagine that Mark Twain is not Samuel Clemens.
> I can not now imagine that Samuel Clemens is not Samuel Clemens.
> Therefore, Mark Twain is not Samuel Clemens.

Translating this argument into forms, we have the same form as for Descartes' argument. Fa, $\sim Fb$, therefore $a = b$. In this case, the conclusion seems straightforwardly false: Mark Twain is (or was) Samuel Clemens! It is not that there are two different people: Mark Twain on the one hand and the Samuel Clemens. (Samuel Clemens is alone in the room – how many people are there? Two? Surely not.) However, the premises seem true. I can imagine a situation in which Mark Twain is not Samuel Clemens. I cannot imagine a situation in which the Samuel Clemens is not Samuel Clemens. What is the matter with the argument?

Opaque contexts

There seems to be a tension between admitting that statements of the form

> I cannot imagine that x exists.
> I cannot imagine that x is not Samuel Clemens.

and others like them are genuine predications of *x*. According to the definition I gave of predicates in Chapter 8, these are one-place predicates, because when we substitute a name in for *x*, we get a sentence. There is no doubt that this does not fit well with the definition of identity. The problem is one of substitution. The truth or falsity of 'I cannot imagine that *x* exists' depends not only on what object is substituted in the expression, but also on the way the object is presented. Here is another example that illustrates the point:

Superman is called *x* because of his amazing powers.

If I substitute the name Superman in this expression, I get a true statement. If I substitute the name Clark Kent in this expression, I get a false statement, even though Clark Kent and Superman name the same person.

Which statements are true of both Clark Kent and Superman? The following all seem true:

x works for a newspaper.
x knows Lois Lane.
x flies through the skies.
x rescues people in distress.
x can be made weak with judicious uses of kryptonite.
You saw *x* rescue my friends.

Once we know that Clark Kent and Superman are the same person, each of these statements seem true if we plug in the name *Superman* or *Clark Kent*. They may not seem to be true to someone who does not know that fact, but that doesn't mean that they are not true. The last sentence is an interesting case. Suppose you saw Superman rescue my friends. It follows that you saw Clark Kent rescue my friends even if you did not recognise that it was Clark Kent. Sometimes we see things that happen, without being able to describe them completely.

These statements all seem true when you substitute one name and false when you substitute the other:

x is widely known to work for a newspaper.
Lois Lane thinks *x* is stronger than Clark Kent.

> I told you that x has amazing powers.
> You saw that x rescued my friends.

Clark Kent is widely known to work for a newspaper. Superman is not so widely known to work for a newspaper. Lois Lane (at least when she was ignorant of Clark's identity) thought that Superman was stronger than Clark Kent, but she certainly didn't think that Clark was stronger than himself. I might have told you that Superman has amazing powers, but I certainly didn't tell you that Clark Kent has amazing powers. You might have seen that Superman rescued my friends, but you didn't *see that* Clark Kent did, because you did not recognise that he and Superman are one and the same person.

There is a pattern occurring. Each of the problematic sentences relies in some way or other on the particulars of language and the way Superman (Clark Kent) is described, and in people's beliefs about him. Being widely known to work for a newspaper is not genuinely a property of a person. It is a property of a person, given a particular description of that person. The truth of the claim can vary, not only as the person changes, but also as the way they are described changes. This sentence is at most a wide predication of a property of Superman (Clark Kent), not a narrow predication, which picks out a property that he has, invariant of how he is described.

This problem is *often* described as one of *substitution into intentional contexts* (or quantification into intentional contexts, when it is a variable over which we quantify). We are substituting names into belief contexts, knowledge contexts, and other contexts in which we are describing what people think, know, have heard or recognise. (These are called *intentional* contexts, because the characteristic property of 'aboutness' is *often* called the *intentionality* of these mental states.) In each case, we want information not only about which object is in question, but also the way that the object is presented or described. These are general contexts into which names can be substituted to form propositions, but they are not predicates in the narrow sense.

In general, a context into which a name can be substituted to form a proposition but that depends not only on the thing denoted is called *opaque*. Belief and knowledge statements and other intentional terms give rise to opaque contexts, but there are other opaque contexts that are not intentional. We have some trivial examples involving quotation marks:

'x' contains eight letters.

Substituting *Superman* for x gives us a truth. Substituting *Clark Kent* gives us a falsehood. This gives us an opaque context involving no mental states.

There is no widely accepted general theory concerning the division between opaque contexts and those that are not opaque (these are sometimes called transparent). To tell the difference, substitute different names for the same object, to check to see if any difference is registered. The distinction is very important, for our assumption in developing predicate logic is that all predicates are transparent. To formalise an argument properly using predicate logic, this assumption must hold. If it does not, then the formalisation is incorrect.

This brings us back to Descartes' argument for dualism. We have formalised it as a simple argument from Fa and $\sim Fb$ to $a = b$, where Fx is *I can now imagine x not existing*. It seems that we have reason to believe that this context is opaque. My capacity to imagine x's existence or non-existence depends on how x is described or presented to me. If that is the case then the formalisation fails to adequately describe the argument. The validity of the argument form from Fa and $\sim Fb$ to $a = b$ tells us nothing about Descartes' argument. To show that his argument is valid, much more must be done.

Further reading

See Chapter 4 of Read's *Thinking about Logic* [21], and Chapter 3 of Grayling's *Introduction to Philosophical Logic* [8] for more on substitution into opaque contexts.

Exercises

Basic

{14.1} Divide the following forms into those that *narrowly* predicate and those that only *widely* predicate (that is, sort them out into *transparent* and *opaque* contexts), and explain your answers in each case (in each case, substitute in names for x):

1   x runs very fast.
2   x is famous for running very fast.
3   x is Prime Minister.
4   x caused the *Titanic* to sink.
5   x is very old.
6   I am sick and tired of x.
7   x did that well.
8   I can't tell the difference between x and y.
9   I know x.

{14.2} Why might it be bad to formalise *I think that something bit me* as $(\exists x)Tx$ where Tx is 'I think that x bit me'?

Advanced

{14.3} Some people think that the problem of quantifying in odd contexts is not restricted to beliefs or other things involving people. Try this argument:

> Necessarily, 9 is bigger than 7.
> 9 is the number of planets.
> Therefore, necessarily, the number of planets is bigger than 7.

Is this valid? If so, does it prove that there must be more than seven planets? If it isn't valid, why isn't it?

> Chi Wen Tzu always thought three times before taking action.
> Twice would have been enough.
> – Confucius

211

Chapter 15

What is logic?

Sometimes the answers you get with classical logic are odd, and not for reasons of vagueness or relevance, and not because of non-denoting terms, or opaque contexts. Here is an example:

The Prime Minister collects clocks.
Anyone who collects clocks has to be slightly mad.
Therefore, someone is slightly mad.

We can use the dictionary

$Mx = x$ is a Prime Minister
$Cx = x$ collects clocks
$Sx = x$ is slightly mad
$Px = x$ is a person

to find the form. The argument has $(Ix)(Mx,Cx)$ and $(\forall x)((Px$ & $Cx) \supset Sx))$ as premises, and the conclusion is $(\exists x)(Px$ & $Sx)$. It is straightforward to show that it is invalid. One counterexample can be found here:

	$I(M)$	$I(C)$	$I(P)$	$I(S)$
a	1	1	0	1

What does the counterexample mean? One assumption in the model is that *the Prime Minister* is not a person. However, the Prime Minister *is* a person – and in fact, the Prime Minister *must* be a person. That is how Australia's constitution is written: you cannot be a prime minister without being a citizen, and you cannot be a citizen without being a person. So, the counterexample is not a possible state of affairs. This is why we might think that the argument is valid. There's no way for the premises to be true and the conclusion to be false. So, is it valid or not?

There is no general agreement on this issue. There are two major lines of thought, and I will consider them in turn.

Logic as invariance under permutation

First, there is the 'No' case. According to the 'No' case, the argument is not valid because we can construct a counterexample. We have displayed two different counterexamples. Logic has to do with the validity of the form of the argument, and the form is what we discovered. According to this view, the validity of the argument is due to the form the argument takes:

> An argument is valid if and only if there is no counterexample to the argument under any interpretation of the non-logical symbols occurring in the argument.

So, to test for the validity of the argument, you take away all of the non-logical parts of the argument (anything other than the connectives, quantifiers and identity), replacing the rest by schematic letters. The search for a counterexample to the argument is then a search for how we might interpret the non-logical parts of the argument in order to make the premises true and the conclusion false. If we cannot find any way to do this, the argument is valid. If we can find such a way, the argument is not valid.

Here is another example. The proposition 'It is raining or it is not raining' is a tautology because it has the form $p \lor \sim p$, and any instance of this form is true. There is no way to substitute any proposition in for p in the statement $p \lor \sim p$ to get a falsehood. For if p is true, $p \lor \sim p$ is true, and if p is not true, $\sim p$ is true, and hence $p \lor \sim p$ is true.

So, according to this account of logical validity, each model is a reinterpretation of the non-logical parts of the argument. If no matter how the non-logical parts are reinterpreted, you never have the premises true and the conclusion false, the argument is valid. This view can be summarised simply:

> Logical validity is *truth preservation in virtue of logical form.*

If truth is preserved from the premises to the conclusion of the argument, in virtue of the form, then the argument is valid.

To get the conclusion from the premises in our original argument, you have to use something other than the form of the argument. You must appeal to the meanings of Prime Minister and of 'person' – specifically, that any Prime Minister is a person. But that gives us a way to repair the argument. If we add a new premise, namely $(\forall x)(Mx \supset Px)$, the new argument is valid.

This new proposition we add is called an *enthymeme*. It is a 'hidden premise', which everyone agrees with, and which when added to the premises of an argument will render the argument valid.

There are a number of significant virtues of this account of logical validity:

A good fit with logical practice

This account fits well with what we do in practice in formal logic. We take the formal structure of the argument, and we reinterpret the non-logical parts of the argument in any way we see fit.

No mysterious necessity

Any account of logic has to postulate some degree of necessity. The premises have to get you to the conclusion in general. This is achieved in this account of logic, not by postulating a mysterious notion of necessity, but by requiring that the argument preserve truth, no matter how the non-logical language is interpreted. The necessity of logic is a matter of its *generality*.

Topic neutrality

Logic is topic-neutral. It applies to anything we can talk about. The fact that logical validity is explicitly defined in terms of arbitrary substitutions of terms means that this account of logic is well placed to explain that fact about the generality and topic neutrality of logical validity.

Logic as necessary truth preservation

Not everyone is happy with this account of validity. According to the 'Yes' case, all this talk about enthymemes is merely fixing up what formal logic gets wrong. According to this view, logic is not primarily about form – for a slogan:

> Logical validity is a matter of necessary truth preservation.

This definition of validity says nothing about forms. For this account of validity, formal techniques are at most a useful tool for giving us insight into what may or may not be possible. On this account, anything that is *formally valid* will be valid, but not everything that is formally invalid is *really* invalid. Not every model will represent a genuine possibility. Models are tools that bring possibilities to light. In our case, the model to make the premises true and the conclusion false isn't a possibility, because of the connection between being Prime Minister and being a person. Once we have ruled out that kind of model, the tree shows us that the argument is valid. There is no way for the premises to be true and the conclusion false. In other cases, a formal construction of a counterexample will bring to light something we recognise to be a possibility, and in these cases we will see that the argument is invalid. At heart, on this view, logic is a tool to be used.

This view has a number of advantages too:

No need for a logical/non-logical distinction

There is no general agreement as to what a distinction between logical and non-logical connectives might be. If validity is a matter of necessary truth preservation, there are valid inferences that depend on the nature of all sorts of other connectives, such as necessity and possibility, counterfactual conditionals, temporal operators such as 'yesterday' and 'tomorrow', colour terms, and many other things. Each term has its part to play in validity. There is no distinction between the logical and the non-logical, except that the commonly used logical connectives are simpler to work with.

Closer fit with pre-theoretical practice

Before we theorised about logical validity, we had a sense that valid arguments were those that made the conclusion sure, given the premises. This view makes that pre-theoretic belief explicit. The way to show that an argument is invalid is to show that you could have the premises true and the conclusion false. It is not to show that if you interpreted one term by something very much different, you get a counterexample. That seems irrelevant to the task of judging the validity of an argument.

Finally, we should note that there are a number of problems remaining with both views. For the view that takes validity to be necessary truth preservation, much more has to be said about the nature of necessity and how we could ever come to know that something is necessary or that something is possible. For the first view, you must modify the account to deal with the quantifiers. The sentence $(\exists x)(\exists y)(x \neq y)$ contains no non-logical vocabulary at all. It is true. There is no reinterpretation of any non-logical vocabulary possible, so it should be a tautology, according to the letter of the law. However, it is not, as we could have a domain of one object. To use the reinterpretation strategy, not only must we reinterpret the non-logical terms, but we also need to be able to reinterpret the ranges of the quantifiers.

Despite this disagreement about the logical validity, there is a great deal of agreement about the usefulness of logical techniques. Disagreement is strongest on the issue of how those techniques work.

Further Reading

This topic is very much a current research issue in the philosophy of logic. Chapter 2 of Read's *Thinking about Logic* [21] and Chapter 2 of Grayling's *An Introduction to Philosophical Logic* [8] provide helpful introductions to the debate. John Etchemendy's *The Concept of Logical Consequence* [5] is a clear and extended treatment of the issue.

> 'Contrariwise,' continued Tweedledee,
> 'If it was so, it might be;
> and if it were so, it would be:
> but as it isn't, it ain't.
> That's logic.'
> – Lewis Carroll

Bibliography

[1] George Boolos and Richard Jeffrey. *Computability and Logic*, 3rd edn. Oxford University Press, Oxford, 1989.

[2] David Bostock. *Intermediate Logic*. Oxford University Press, Oxford, 1997.

[3] Brian F. Chellas. *Modal Logic: An Introduction*. Cambridge University Press, Cambridge, 1980.

[4] Michael Dummett. *Elements of Intuitionism*. Oxford University Press, Oxford, 1977.

[5] John Etchemendy. *The Concept of Logical Consequence*. Harvard University Press, Cambridge, MA, 1990.

[6] Graeme Forbes. *Modern Logic*. Oxford University Press, Oxford, 1994.

[7] Bas van Fraassen. Presuppositions, supervaluations and free logic. In: Karel Lambert, (ed.), *The Logical Way of Doing Things*. Yale University Press, New Haven, CT, 1969.

[8] A. C. Grayling. *An Introduction to Philosophical Logic*, 3rd edn. Blackwell, Oxford, 1997.

[9] H. P. Grice. Logic and conversation. In: P. Cole and J. L. Morgan (ed.), *Syntax and Semantics: Speech Acts*, Volume 3, pages 41–58. Academic Press, New York, 1975. Reprinted in Jackson [14].

[10] Susan Haack. *Deviant Logic, Fuzzy Logic: Beyond the Formalism*. Cambridge University Press, Cambridge, 1996.

[11] Arend Heyting. *Intuitionism: An Introduction*. North-Holland, Amsterdam, 1956.

[12] Colin Howson. *Logic with Trees: An Introduction to Symbolic Logic*. Routledge, London, 1996.

[13] G. Hughes and M. Cresswell. *A New Introduction to Modal Logic*. Routledge, London, 1996.

[14] Frank Jackson. *Conditionals*. Oxford Readings in Philosophy, Oxford University Press, Oxford, 1991.

[15] E. J. Lemmon. *Beginning Logic*. Nelson, London, 1965.

[16] David K. Lewis. *Counterfactuals*. Blackwell, Oxford, 1973.

[17] —— *On the Plurality of Worlds*. Blackwell, Oxford, 1986.

[18] Jan Łukasiewicz. On determinism. In: L. Borkowski, (ed.), *Selected Works*. North-Holland, Amsterdam, 1970.

[19] Alexander Miller. *Philosophy of Language*. Fundamentals of Philosophy, UCL Press, London, 1998.

[20] Dag Prawitz. *Natural Deduction: A Proof Theoretical Study*. Almqvist and Wiksell, Stockholm, 1965.

[21] Stephen Read. *Thinking about Logic*. Oxford University Press, Oxford, 1995.

[22] Greg Restall. *An Introduction to Substructural Logics*. Routledge, London, 2000.

[23] Richard Routley. Some things do not exist. *Notre Dame Journal of Formal Logic*, 7:251–276, 1966.

[24] Bertrand Russell. On denoting. *Mind*, 14, 1905.

[25] R. M. Sainsbury. *Logical Forms: An Introduction to Philosophical Logic*. Blackwell, Oxford, 1991.

[26] Gila Sher. *The Bounds of Logic*. MIT Press, Cambridge, MA, 1991.

[27] John K. Slaney. Vagueness revisited. Technical Report TR–ARP–15/88, Automated Reasoning Project, Australian National University, Canberra, 1988.

[28] John K. Slaney. A general logic. *Australasian Journal of Philosophy*, 68:74–88, 1990.

[29] R. M. Smullyan. *First-Order Logic*. Springer-Verlag, Berlin, 1968. Reprinted by Dover Press, New York, 1995.

[30] A. S. Troelstra and H. Schwichtenberg. *Basic Proof Theory*. Cambridge Tracts in Theoretical Computer Science, Volume 43, Cambridge University Press, Cambridge, 1996.

[31] Timothy Williamson. *Vagueness*. Routledge, London, 1994.

Index

CPSIA information can be obtained at www.ICGtesting.com
Printed in the USA
LVOW04s0739121114

413166LV00004B/29/P